URBAN PHYSICAL EDUCATION

Instructional Practices and Cultural Activities

Rhonda L. Clements

Amy Meltzer Rady

Human Kinetics

Library of Congress Cataloging-in-Publication Data

Clements, Rhonda L.
  Urban physical education : instructional practices and cultural activities / Rhonda L. Clements, Amy Meltzer Rady.
    p. cm.
  Includes bibliographical references and index.
  ISBN-13: 978-0-7360-9839-7 (soft cover)
  ISBN-10: 0-7360-9839-9 (soft cover)
  1. Physical education and training. 2. Education, Urban. I. Meltzer Rady, Amy, 1953- II. Title.
  GV341.C5559 2012
  613.7--dc23

                  2011032913

ISBN-10: 0-7360-9839-9 (print)

ISBN-13: 978-0-7360-9839-7 (print)

The web addresses cited in this text were current as of October 2011, unless otherwise noted.

Acquisitions Editor: Scott Wikgren; **Developmental Editor:** Ray Vallese; **Assistant Editor:** Derek Campbell; **Copyeditor:** Joyce Sexton; **Indexer:** Sharon Duffy; **Permissions Manager:** Dalene Reeder; **Graphic Designer:** Fred Starbird; **Graphic Artist:** Angela K. Snyder; **Cover Designer:** Keith Blomberg; **Photographer (cover):** Photos courtesy of Roy Groething; **Photographer (interior):** Photos courtesy of Roy Groething, unless otherwise noted; photos on pp. 13, 38, and 42 © Human Kinetics; photo on p. 4 © AP Photo/The Wheeling (W.Va.) News-Register, John Wickline; photo on p. 17 © AP Photo/The Las Vegas Sun, Steve Marcus; photos on pp. 36 and 45 © AP Photo/Ric Francis; **Photo Asset Manager:** Laura Fitch; **Visual Production Assistant:** Joyce Brumfield; **Photo Production Manager:** Jason Allen; **Art Manager:** Kelly Hendren; **Associate Art Manager:** Alan L. Wilborn; **Illustrations:** © Human Kinetics; **Printer:** Versa Press

Printed in the United States of America

10 9 8 7 6 5 4 3 2 1

The paper in this book is certified under a sustainable forestry program.

Human Kinetics
Website: www.HumanKinetics.com

United States: Human Kinetics
P.O. Box 5076
Champaign, IL 61825-5076
800-747-4457
e-mail: humank@hkusa.com

Canada: Human Kinetics
475 Devonshire Road Unit 100
Windsor, ON N8Y 2L5
800-465-7301 (in Canada only)
e-mail: info@hkcanada.com

Europe: Human Kinetics
107 Bradford Road
Stanningley
Leeds LS28 6AT, United Kingdom
+44 (0) 113 255 5665
e-mail: hk@hkeurope.com

Australia: Human Kinetics
57A Price Avenue
Lower Mitcham, South Australia 5062
08 8372 0999
e-mail: info@hkaustralia.com

New Zealand: Human Kinetics
P.O. Box 80
Torrens Park, South Australia 5062
0800 222 062
e-mail: info@hknewzealand.com

E5245

CONTENTS

ACTIVITY FINDER

Title of the activity	Primary place of origin	Page
Ace, King, Queen, or Jack	Ireland and urban settings worldwide	120
African Bolo Ball	Africa	54
Blister	United States and urban settings worldwide	125
Chinese Soccer	China	61
Culturally Diverse Cooperative Challenges	Sweden, Italy, Jamaica, Egypt, England, Switzerland, Ireland, Greece, United States	72
Culturally Diverse Fitness Challenges	Germany, China, Brazil, Portugal, United States, Japan, Spain, England, Greece, Egypt	77
Culturally Diverse Race Challenges	England, Greece, Italy, Australia, New Zealand, Ireland, Belgium	79
Culturally Diverse Stretching and Exercise Challenges	Japan, Africa, United States, Mexico, Peru, Sweden, Germany, Greece, China	74
Egyptian Group Bowling	Egypt	56
El Circulo Handball	Spain	58
Finnish Baseball or Pesapallo	Finland	69
Fives	Ireland	57
Four Goals Futbal	Peru	65
Four-Team Rip Flag Challenge	Netherlands	66
Freestyle Basketball Ball-Handling Skills	United States and urban settings worldwide	87
The Harlem Shake	United States	132
Hotshot Hoops	United States and urban settings worldwide	95
Inner-City Workout: Beat Down	United States and urban settings worldwide	112
Italian Fence or Palificata	Italy	63

PREFACE

The possibility of school budget cuts or hiring freezes can cause even the most experienced physical education teacher in an affluent school district to feel anxious. Imagine teaching in a school where the myriad challenges include not only limited finances and a shortage of teachers but also inadequate equipment for large class sizes, daily classroom management problems, school violence, a high percentage of non-English-speaking students, and a variety of ongoing serious student social issues. These working conditions are a reality and are not likely to improve in the near future.

Challenges such as these are part of the daily plight for many urban middle and high school physical education teachers throughout the United States, and they are becoming more prevalent in suburban and rural school settings. *Urban Physical Education: Instructional Practices and Cultural Activities* targets these adverse teaching circumstances and related conditions and presents innovative instructional practices and cultural physical activities for today's changing and varied student demographics. This book also assists teachers in generating a new level of student enthusiasm and participation.

Urban Physical Education enables teachers to gain a better understanding of issues within most schools located in urban settings. It follows a logical progression of content beginning with information that will help teachers learn how to

* enhance their teaching presence and organizational skills;
* acquire and implement teaching suggestions from experienced urban teachers;
* implement instructional practices aimed at the realities of challenging school environments;
* have positive interactions with difficult students and better reinforce classroom protocols;
* convey the importance of respecting human differences through individual, partner, and whole-group cultural games and sport activities;

* add numerous innovative physical activities to the existing curriculum even if the budget is limited and class sizes are large; and
* assess a lesson's success even when working with large groups and limited resources and equipment.

Part one of the book identifies common challenges facing today's urban physical education teachers and offers six instructional practices that coincide with the concept of *culturally responsive teaching*. Among other factors, culturally responsive teaching takes into account the student's race, ethnic origin, and linguistic and academic background and addresses the needs of English language learners. Part one also focuses on the urban physical education teacher as a leader. It emphasizes suggestions for strengthening one's teaching demeanor, conveying life skills, responding to individual behavioral problems as well as issues related to school gangs, and implementing protocols for large class sizes.

Part two offers cultural activities (e.g., games or modified sports recognized in various parts of the world) that can provide students with a culturally diverse environment conforming to the National Association for Sport and Physical Education (NASPE) 2009 instructional practice guidelines. This part gives key information needed to implement these activities by providing a brief description of the origin and purpose of each activity, a simplified teaching process, key instructional points, and a basic closure question for the teacher to pose to students following their participation.

Part two also offers a variety of contemporary sport and performance activities of special interest to students living in urban areas. These activities include urban dances, parkour, urban golf, freestyle basketball and soccer skills, and novel urban fitness routines.

The book's final chapter presents four rubrics that can be used in large classes with limited equipment and difficult learning environments. One sample rubric can be used by teacher trainers when preparing teachers to teach in diverse school settings. Another appraises the extent of positive socialization that a student experiences while interacting with a partner or peer. The third rubric measures the individual's success while interacting with a group of peers. The fourth rubric assesses the extent to which an entire class has achieved the teacher's primary objectives or outcomes.

Finally, the appendix contains definitions of terms and concepts in urban settings; agencies to help teachers address the high incidence of social problems such as teen alcoholism, teenage preg-

nancy, bullying, teenage suicide, and drug abuse; and the national standards for physical education.

Urban Physical Education offers teachers many considerations for multiethnic and urban physical education settings. Teachers can use the book to develop or reinforce existing urban teaching practices, expand their understanding and performance of cultural games and sport activities, and enhance an existing traditional curriculum with innovative and contemporary middle and high school activities.

ACKNOWLEDGMENTS

The authors express their appreciation to many individuals in the West New York School District in New Jersey for their cooperation in having their students demonstrate activities discussed in this book and in permitting us to photograph the students performing those activities. We give special thanks to John Fauta, the district's superintendent of schools; Robert Sanchez, assistant superintendent of schools; Scott Cannao, Memorial High School principal; Silverio Vega, athletic director; John Fraraccio, district supervisor of Heath and Physical Education; and the following participating students: M. Leon, B. Lecea, K. Furlong, T. Saurborn, J. Toribio, T. Quito, F. Aquilar, J. Fonseca, A. Carpio, A. Russell, R. Lewis Jr., F. Abbasi, and M. Zapata. We extend our thanks to William Paterson University's kinesiology students Bellal Awadallah, Christopher Anzano, Laurence Livingston, and Saul Garcia, who assisted in the photography session. We express our gratitude to Roy Groething, who is responsible for many of the photographs in this book.

We also express our appreciation to the many WPU undergraduate kinesiology majors who field tested several of the multicultural games and urban activities identified in this book. We acknowledge Suzanne Kinzler for sharing her invaluable expertise regarding this resource's rubrics and her ongoing professional support in field testing several of the physical education cultural challenges. Ms. Kinzler is a health education teacher in Jersey City, New Jersey.

We would like to thank Sarajane Quinn (acquisitions editor at Human Kinetics) for her early suggestions regarding the design and purpose of this book. We also thank Scott Wikgren (director of Health, Physical Education, Recreation, and Dance at Human Kinetics) for his enthusiasm and excitement about our ideas for this book. In addition, we commend Ray Vallese (senior developmental editor at Human Kinetics) for his guidance through the revisions.

Special thanks are extended to Sylvia J. Giallombardo, Arnold Rady, and Evelyn Meltzer for their ongoing support and inspiration for this book.

PART ONE

CONSIDERATIONS FOR PHYSICAL EDUCATION TEACHERS IN URBAN SETTINGS

CHAPTER 1

CULTURALLY RESPONSIVE TEACHING PRACTICES

Teachers employed in large urban schools are familiar with the term *working in the trenches*. Large urban schools have long been characterized as having below-average workplace conditions, low socioeconomic student status associated with "at-risk" students, rundown facilities, and a scarcity of equipment. They are also known for their high turnover rate, high student absenteeism and dropout rates, overly crowded classrooms, behavioral management problems, lack of parental involvement, and highly disruptive surrounding neighborhoods and community violence.

Some state and city departments of education use preferred terms when identifying these schools. For example, New York City's Department of Education refers to these urban schools as *high-need schools*, and Chicago's urban teachers are recognized for their work in "hard-to-staff" schools. Some administrators and media groups prefer the terms *schools of underserved youth, economically disadvantaged schools, inner-city schools, Title I schools*, or *low-income schools*. Many politicians and the U.S. Department of Education's National Center for Education Statistics (2010) use the term *high-poverty schools* when reporting research findings to the public. Regardless of the variety of words, concepts, or even pejorative terms associated with many urban school settings, urban teachers have found ways to strengthen their teaching effectiveness by implementing teaching practices linked to the term *culturally responsive teaching*.

What Do We Mean by High-Need School?

A high-need school is a school that faces unique challenges when charged with increasing student achievement. The high-need determination is often made through the calculation of a peer index. Where a school falls on this peer index scale helps to determine how high need the school actually is in comparison with other schools. An elementary school's peer index is calculated using a composite demographic statistic based on the percentages of English language learners, special education students, and Black and Hispanic students, as well as eligibility for Title I free and reduced lunch. Middle and high schools' peer index is calculated using the average 4th- or 8th-grade proficiency ratings for English language arts and math.

Culturally responsive teaching in the physical education setting involves more than having students learn about other cultures or develop an appreciation for their own heritage. Nor is it merely having groups of students participate in

What Do We Mean by At-Risk?

Over time, the term *at-risk* has been used to identify students who share several common characteristics. These students are often children of immigrants who do not speak English in the home setting. Often, the individual has very limited English proficiency or is bilingual. At-risk students can also come from a minority population. Their mothers may have had limited education; their home environment as well as their neighborhood may be characterized by poverty; or both of these conditions may exist. Many of the children have been reared in neighborhoods known for a high crime and violence rate. School dropout rates are obviously higher for at-risk students.

ing that all teachers have a responsibility to teach and convey Standard American English, and (d) offer additional partner and cooperative learning activities. However, the overall lack of information on preferred learning styles for different cultural groups is a great concern. This chapter discusses six culturally responsive teaching practices to assist physical education teachers in filling in a small portion of the specialized knowledge needed to be a highly effective teacher of diverse student populations:

1. Recognize cultural characteristics reflecting race and ethnicity.
2. Become acquainted with students' native countries.
3. Recognize intercultural differences in gestures and body language.
4. Address the needs of English language learners.

a series of games from other countries or understand how to manipulate a piece of sport equipment from another nation. Culturally responsive teaching stresses the need for teachers to take into account the student's race and ethnic origin as well as linguistic and academic background, since one's culture can influence a preferred learning style, communication patterns, values and partiality toward specific physical activities and sport, and orientation to school. For example, research performed in the classroom focusing on cultural learning styles for African American students showed that many prefer more kinesthetic or tactile learning and rely heavily on visual input rather than auditory input. Some African American students speak Black English vernacular or Ebonics, which is a language system characteristic of certain African American communities in urban areas and particularly in southern states. Small-group discussions among African American peer groups often result in simultaneous talk instead of alternating talk with pauses, and individuals also prefer maintaining proximity to other peers.

To apply this information on cultural learning style preference to physical education, African American students might benefit more from teachers who (a) provide greater opportunities for physical movement in the gymnasium, (b) offer additional opportunities to engage in interactive health-related discussions, (c) view Ebonics as a cultural trait and not a deficiency while still realiz-

Metal detectors, police officers, and other safety measures have become common sights in many urban schools.

Composition of Student Bodies in Urban Schools

Unlike most countries where education is under the auspices of the federal government, schooling in the United States is not a national function. Each state is legally responsible for education, and local districts are held accountable for the children's education. In 2010 there were nearly 64 million children entering public and private schools. Thirty-five percent of these children were from minority households, and one in five students came from another country. Nearly one-fifth came from homes classified as having poverty-level incomes. The 120 largest school districts in the United States serve 11 million students. All of these schools are defined as urban schools.

5. Use nondiscriminatory selection techniques, international skill practice formations, and urban ways to start a game.

6. Enhance the learning environment with themed bulletin boards and greetings.

PRACTICE 1:
Recognize Cultural Characteristics Reflecting Race and Ethnicity

Culturally responsive instruction places importance on teachers' ability to distinguish between cultural traits and gestures and those that are a matter of individual personality or preference. This is a very difficult task since many urban classes comprise students who have recently immigrated to this country.

To begin, a teacher should be knowledgeable about the student's race and ethnicity. The term *race* is used to identify a person's genetic heritage. Physical characteristics usually include one's skin color, hair characteristics, facial and eye features, height, and other physical aspects of appearance that are generally hereditary. The term *ethnic-*

ity is used to discuss one's cultural background and birth origin. In the United States, the Office of Management and Budget (OMB) oversees the standards that govern the categories used to collect and present federal data on race and ethnicity. These recognized standards identify the following five categories concerning one's race: American Indian or Alaska Native, Asian, Black or African American, Native Hawaiian or Other Pacific Islander, and White. Teachers should note that a student's Hispanic origin is an ethnicity rather than a race, and therefore persons of Hispanic origin may be of any race. Hispanics trace their heritage to countries that were colonized by Spain and continue to use Spanish as an official language. These countries include: Argentina, Bolivia, Chile, Colombia, Costa Rica, Cuba, Dominican Republic, Ecuador, El Salvador, Equatorial Guinea, Guatemala, Honduras, Mexico, Nicaragua, Panama, Paraguay, Peru, Puerto Rico, Spain, Uruguay, and Venezuela.

Overall, these racial and ethnic categories are helpful to a teacher's understanding while still recognizing that a blurring of racial lines can be expected to occur over time as more children are born to interracial couples.

Racial groupings are as follows (U.S. Department of Education, National Center for Education Statistics 2010):

* *American Indian or Alaska Native:* A student having origins in any of the original peoples of North and South America (including Central America) who maintains tribal affiliation or community attachment

* *Asian:* A student having origins in any of the original peoples of the Far East, Southeast Asia, and the Indian subcontinent, for example, Cambodia, China, India, Japan, Korea, Malaysia, Pakistan, the Philippines, Thailand, and Vietnam

* *Black:* A student having origins in any of the Black racial groups of Africa

* *Native Hawaiian or Other Pacific Islander:* A student having origins in any of the original peoples of Hawaii, Guam, Samoa, or other Pacific Islands

* *White:* A student having origins in any of the original peoples of Europe, North Africa, or the Middle East

* *Two or more races:* A student who selected two or more of the following racial categories when offered the option of selecting one or

more racial designations: White, Black, Asian, Native Hawaiian or Other Pacific Islander, or American Indian or Alaska Native

Ethnicity is categorized as follows (U.S. Department of Education, National Center for Education Statistics 2010):

* *Hispanic or Latino:* A student of Cuban, Mexican, Puerto Rican, South or Central American, or other Spanish culture or origin, regardless of race

Most metropolitan areas and most countries are composed of several ethnic minority groups. These minority groups share similar language, origins, and types of preferred foods, as well as lifestyles that differ from that of the majority of the overall population. Urban physical education teachers in the United States often find themselves working with students from several different races and ethnic groups.

Throughout most of its history, the United States has had influxes of immigration. The ethnic mix of immigrants is 83 percent white (generally of European descent, but also from the Middle East and Latin America), 12 percent African American, 3 percent Asian, and about 1 percent Native American. Today the largest immigrant groups are from Latin countries. These statistics support the notion that our classrooms comprise students with diverse ethnic backgrounds and mixed performance levels.

PRACTICE 2:
Become Acquainted With Students' Native Countries

Working with recent immigrants is very likely given that more than 30 states have at least one of the 100 largest school districts. These include Florida (14); Texas (14); California (11); Georgia (6); Maryland (5); Louisiana, North Carolina, Tennessee, Utah, and Virginia (4 each); Ohio (3); and Arizona, Colorado, Minnesota, Nevada, and New York (2 each). The following states each have one: Alabama, Alaska, Hawaii, Illinois, Kansas, Kentucky, Massachusetts, Michigan, Missouri, New Mexico, Oregon, Pennsylvania, South Carolina, Washington, and Wisconsin.

Implementing culturally responsive instruction places importance on the teacher's having some understanding of a student's native country. Ideally, this would include knowing a variety of facts about the country's primary language; the density of the population; characteristics of the land and climate; national holidays; religious, social, and political influences; common first names and surnames; and relationships among family members.

This can be very difficult to achieve in urban schools that have more than 20 different cultures in a single class. In these cases, urban physical education teachers can still benefit from being genuinely interested in the location of the native country of a student or group of students, identifying the national sports and recreational pastimes in that country, and learning what sport activity from their background students most favor. Conversations with students can also uncover cultural differences and similarities regarding the country's favorite foods and eating habits.

One of the most frequent questions that teachers ask a new student is "Where are you from?" since the information is a starting point for learning more about the student's previous educational experiences. The following information can help the teacher gain a clearer geographical understanding about a student's origin.

* *Asia:* Afghanistan, Azerbaijan, Bahrain, Bangladesh, China, Georgia, India, Iran, Iraq, Kazakhstan, Kuwait, Lebanon, Pakistan, Russia, Saudi Arabia, Sri Lanka, Turkey
* *Africa:* Algeria, Angola, Cameroon, Egypt, Ethiopia, Ghana, Kenya, Libya, Morocco, Nigeria, Senegal, South Africa, Tanzania
* *Europe:* Austria, Belgium, Bulgaria, Croatia, Cyprus, Czech Republic, Denmark, Estonia, Finland, France, Germany, Greece, Hungary, Ireland, Italy, Latvia, Lithuania, Luxembourg, Netherlands, Norway, Poland, Portugal, Romania, Slovakia, Slovenia, Spain, Sweden, United Kingdom, Ukraine
* *North and South America:* Argentina, Bolivia, Brazil, Canada, Chile, Colombia, Dominican Republic, Ecuador, Salvador, Jamaica, Mexico, The Bahamas, United States, Venezuela
* *East Asia and Australasia (includes Islands of the South Pacific):* Australia, Brunei, Cambodia, Hong Kong, Indonesia, Japan, Malaysia, New Guinea, New Zealand, Philippines, Singapore, South Korea, Taiwan, Thailand, Vietnam

Likewise, a student's first name can give a teacher a quick indication where the student is from. In many cultures, first names are reused to commemorate ancestors or people who are particularly admired and well known for their accomplishments. For example, Hebrew names are most often derived from the early parts of the Bible. See table 1.1 for popular names in selected countries.

It is also beneficial when the teacher is familiar with other countries' national sports and leisure activities (see table 1.2). Using this information, the teacher can appear genuinely interested in a student's previous sport experiences.

PRACTICE 3:
Recognize Intercultural Differences in Gestures and Body Language

A person's body language is a form of unspoken communication or message that is conveyed non-verbally to another individual or group of people. A student's body language in a physical education setting often conveys a personal preference or agreement or disagreement, or indicates how a student is feeling (e.g., engrossed, indifferent, or

Table 1.1 Popular Names Throughout the World

Country	Boys' names	Girls' names
Australia	Benjamin, Ethan, Jack, Joshua, Lachlan, Thomas, William, Samuel	Chloe, Ella, Emily, Emma, Olivia, Sophie
Brazil	Gabriel, Gustavo, Giulherme, Mateus, Vitor	Anna, Eduarda, Gabriela, Girvanna, Isabela, Julia, Maria, Marie
Canada	Ethan, Jacob, Joshua, Matthew, Nathan, Samuel, Thomas	Emma, Emily, Hannah, Madison, Sarah
Chile	Benjamin, Mathias, Martin, Sabastian, Vicente	Constanza, Catalina, Javiera, Martina, Valentina
China	Chen, Jian, Li, Tai	Bo, Jia, Lin, Mulan, Mei
Croatia	Luka, Ivan, Marko, Karlo	Ana, Emma, Lana, Lucija, Petra
Finland	Filip, Jonaines, Johannes, Juhani, Marko, Matias, Mikael, Karlo, Olavi	Maria, Emilia, Sofia, Aino, Olivia
France	Enzo, Mathis, Lucas, Hugo, Matheo	Clara, Chloe, Emma, Lea, Manon, Sarah
Germany	Maximillian, Leon, Lukas, Flynn	Anna, Leonie, Marie, Maria, Sophie
India	Damian, Arnav, Nilay, Taj	Avani, Eva, Maliha, Bela
Japan	Yuuki, Haruto, Souta, Yuuto, Haruki	Yui, Harika
Russia	Alexandr, Andrey, Daniil, Dmitry, Ivan	Alexandra, Alina, Anna, Anastasia, Ekateria
Spain	Alejandro, Daniel, Pablo, David, Javier	Laura, Lucia, Maria, Paula, Marta
United Kingdom	Harry, Joshua, Oliver, Samuel, Thomas, William	Emily, Grace, Jessica, Ruby, Grace
United States	Aiden, Jacob, Ethan, Ryan, Matthew	Emily, Emma, Madison, Abigail, Sophie

Table 1.2 National Sports and Leisure Activities Throughout the World

Country	National sport or pastime
Afghanistan	Buskashi
Andorra	Rugby
Anguilla	Yacht racing
Antigua	Cricket
Bahamas	Sloop sailing
Bangladesh	Kabaddi
Canada	Ice hockey
Chile	Chilean rodeo
China	Table tennis
Colombia	Association football
Cuba	Baseball
Dominican Republic	Baseball
Finland	Pesapallo
Georgia	Rugby
Grenada	Cricket
India	Field hockey
Ireland	Gaelic games
Jamaica	Cricket
Korea	Taekwondo
Latvia	Basketball
Lithuania	Basketball
Mexico	Charreria
New Zealand	Rugby
Norway	Cross-country skiing
Pakistan	Field hockey
Papua New Guinea	Rugby
Peru	Paleta frontón
Philippines	Arnis
Puerto Rico	Paso fino
Turkey	Wrestling and jereed
South Korea	Starcraft
Sri Lanka	Volleyball
United States	Baseball
Uruguay	Gaucho skills
Wales	Rugby

not interested in an activity). Often, a close friend and even a teacher can surmise how a middle school or high school student is feeling about an activity from the individual's body language.

Body language consists of facial expressions, postures, and body gestures. Body gestures are most often used as a way to greet or signal goodbye and may be used to beckon someone. Bowing, for example, is a formal greeting gesture consisting of a slight nod of the head among peers. The greater the respect for the person, the lower the bow. In countries such as Japan, bowing is clearly defined and is an important part of greetings. In the United States, greetings are generally quite informal. For example, most students from the United States greet each other with a casual "Hello" or "How are you?" or "Hi" or even "Hey." In many urban settings it is also acceptable to say "Yo." Students also use some form of handshake when meeting but rarely shake hands upon leaving, and the handshake is usually brief and firm.

Waving is most often with an open palm, flat or slightly curved, and is used to greet people from a distance. Hugging variations include placing the hand on a person's shoulder and applying slight inward pressure, or hugging from the front or side of the body. Hugging is common between females. Males prefer light shoulder-only hugs and side-on or one-handed hugs. Social greetings are relatively short. Students from the United States also maintain eye contact, smile a great deal even at strangers, and like to have their smiles returned. Some students, especially athletes, give others a light slap on the back to show friendship. People from the United States are generally uncomfortable with same-sex touching, especially between males, and holding the middle finger up by itself is considered a vulgar gesture.

Some foreign-born students demonstrate different behavior patterns and body gestures in everyday practices. They can also gesture while performing a physical skill. Differences in body language are also related to a country's culture. For example, the more reserved high school student from the United States has a different concept of personal space than her foreign counterpart. Spanish students tend to stand in close proximity when conversing and use hand gestures and physical contact as a nonverbal language. Italian and French students are usually outwardly affectionate when securing a cooperative goal. Effective physical educators from the United States accept these differences.

Physical education teachers should be aware that they use a variety of nonverbal messages in their communication with students. These messages can emanate from

* body positioning (e.g., the space between the teacher and the student),
* voice (e.g., sound, inflection, volume, pitch, timber),
* tactile behavior (e.g., handshake, pat on the back, shoulder, or head),
* body motion (e.g., waving of arms, pointing with finger or hands, tilting or nodding the head, eye contact, facial expressions), and
* unique sport gestures (e.g., making the OK sign, thumbs up, hands clasped over head in a victory sign, running with both arms in the air as in scoring a goal or basket, high five, and even a complex sport handshake).

Teachers should also be aware of specific gestures to avoid when teaching students of a specific culture.

The following list provides examples of acceptable greeting gestures and information related to personal space. It also identifies particularly rude gestures.

The Handshake in Sports

The handshake originated from the early Romans as a way of greeting and symbolizing the transference of power from one person to another person. Today, athletes or team captains shake hands before a game. There are many possible components of greeting, as the styles vary significantly across social groups and cultures. A firm handshake grip shows confidence. Palm down indicates dominance and a feeling of superiority, and palm sideways indicates equality. Palm up indicates a friendly hello or is used to show submission. Teammates frequently shake or slap hands during a game. Hand touching is also used, for example the "high five," in which open palms are touched high in the air or closed fists are tapped.

Argentina (Argentineans)

* **Acceptable gestures:** A friendly handshake is the custom, and good friends often embrace. Students from Argentina stand close to each other when speaking and frequently touch. To convey "hurry up," people tap their thumb and middle finger together.
* **Rude gestures:** The OK sign and "thumbs up" gesture are considered vulgar. Hitting the palm of the left hand with the right fist means "I don't believe what you are saying" or "That's stupid."

Australia (Australians)

* **Acceptable gestures:** A firm handshake is an acceptable greeting.
* **Rude gestures:** The "V" sign (made with index and middle fingers, palm facing inward) is a very vulgar gesture. The "thumbs up" gesture is also considered obscene.

Austria (Austrians)

* **Acceptable gestures:** Sportsmanlike gestures are highly valued. Austrians are most often reserved and formal. Eye contact is very important, and touching and physical closeness in public are not common.
* **Rude gestures:** Winking at a female is considered improper.

Belgium (Belgians)

* **Acceptable gestures:** When close friends meet they often air kiss three times—once on each cheek and then back to the right cheek. The OK sign means zero.
* **Rude gestures:** It is considered impolite to snap one's fingers. Back slapping is considered offensive. Pointing with the index finger is considered impolite.

Bolivia (Bolivians)

* **Acceptable gestures:** Bolivians stand very close when conversing. Close male friends may embrace, and female students often embrace and touch cheeks. If an individual thinks his hand is dirty, he offers his forearm to shake.
* **Rude gestures:** Teachers can be viewed as untrustworthy if they do not maintain direct eye contact. The "so-so" gesture (rocking your palm-down open hand from side to side) means "no" in Bolivia.

Brazil (Brazilians)

* **Acceptable gestures:** Brazilians stand extremely close to one another. Females in Brazil kiss once on each cheek if they are married, and single women add a third kiss. Physical contact is part of simple communication. Touching arms, elbows, and backs is very common and acceptable.
* **Rude gestures:** The OK sign is considered very vulgar; the "thumbs up" gesture is used for approval. Wiping your hands together means "It doesn't matter." Clicking the tongue and shaking the head indicates disagreement or disapproval.

Canada (Canadians)

* **Acceptable gestures:** Excessive gesturing is not common. Maintaining a certain amount of personal space is important, as is good eye contact. A firm handshake is a customary greeting.
* **Rude gestures:** French Canadians are generally more expressive than other Canadians. In Quebec the "thumbs down" is considered offensive, as is slapping an open palm over a closed fist. French Canadians use the "thumbs up" sign to mean "OK." The OK sign made with the index finger and thumb means zero in Quebec.

Chile (Chileans)

* **Acceptable gestures:** Chileans are expressive people, and they stand closer than North Americans.
* **Rude gestures:** It is rude to snap the fingers at anyone. Students should never be beckoned with an index finger. A chin flick means "I couldn't care less," and hitting the palm of the left hand with the right fist is considered a vulgar gesture.

China (Chinese)

* **Acceptable gestures:** The Chinese dislike being touched by strangers, and teachers should not touch, lock arms, back slap, or make any body contact. Chinese may nod or bow instead of shaking hands, although shaking hands has become increasingly common. When introduced to a Chinese group of students, teachers may be greeted with applause. The individual should applaud back.

Students in the United States often form close huddles and touch hands to express camaraderie, but many common gestures have very different meanings in other countries.

* **Rude gestures:** Snapping the fingers or whistling is considered very rude. To beckon a Chinese student, face the palm of your hand downward and move your fingers in a scratching motion. Teachers should not use their index finger to beckon anyone and never point with the index finger. Chinese point with an open hand.

Colombia (Colombians)

* **Acceptable gestures:** Smiling is very important, and so is a handshake when one is arriving or departing.

* **Rude gestures:** It is considered demeaning to beckon a student with the index finger. Instead, beckon with the palm down, waving the fingers or your whole hand.

Denmark (Danes)

* **Acceptable gestures:** Danes prefer ample personal space and are very reserved about being touched.

* **Rude gestures:** Speaking loudly or suddenly should be avoided.

Ecuador (Ecuadorians)

* **Acceptable gestures:** The handshake is customary for meeting and departing, and there is a good deal of touching among friends and family.

* **Rude gestures:** Fidgeting with hands and feet is distracting and considered very impolite. Holding out a hand as though to shake hands and twisting it back and forth means "no." It is impolite to point at someone. Ecuadorians may point by puckering or pursing their lips.

Finland (Finns)

* **Acceptable gestures:** Finns prefer ample personal space and do not desire to be touched. Maintain eye contact.
* **Rude gestures:** It is rude to have a conversation with one's hands in the pants pocket.

France (French)

* **Acceptable gestures:** The French prefer a light, quick, single handshake. A strong, rhythmic handshake is viewed as unrefined. When family and close friends greet one another, they often air kiss both cheeks. The French seldom smile at strangers in public.
* **Rude gestures:** Slapping the open palm over a closed fist is considered a vulgar gesture. The OK sign, made with index finger and thumb, means zero. The French use the "thumbs up" sign to say "OK."

Germany (Germans)

* **Acceptable gestures:** Germans value order, privacy, and punctuality. Most Germans appear reserved and value their personal space.
* **Rude gestures:** The "thumbs up" gesture means "one" or is a sign of appreciation or agreement. Making hands into two fists, thumbs tucked inside the other fingers, and pounding lightly on a surface expresses "good luck." The OK sign (index finger and thumb joined together to make a circle) is considered a rude gesture. Pointing the index finger to one's own head is considered an insult.

Greece (Greeks)

* **Acceptable gestures:** Greeks are known to smile when they are happy and even when they are upset. They are often affectionate with friends, and their handshake is firm while they maintain eye contact.
* **Rude gestures:** Nodding the head "yes" is not polite; say "yes" instead. The OK sign is a rude gesture; "thumbs up" means OK.

India (Indians)

* **Acceptable gestures:** Indians value personal space and generally allow an arm's-length space between themselves and others. The greeting is the "namaste" (na-mas-TAY), with the palms placed together and held at chest height. This is done in conjunction with a slight bow. Men shake hands with men when meeting or leaving but do not touch women when meeting or greeting.
* **Rude gestures:** Public displays of affection are not considered proper, although Indian males may engage in friendly back patting merely as a sign of friendship. The left hand and the feet are considered unclean. The head is considered sensitive and should not be touched. Indians are very sensitive to being beckoned rudely. Teachers should never point with a single finger or two fingers (used only with inferiors). Instead, pointing is done with an upward tilt of the chin, whole hand, or thumb.

Indonesia (Indonesians)

* **Acceptable gestures:** People greet by saying "Selamat" (sell-a-mat), which means peace. Indonesians shake hands and give a slight nod when meeting for the first time. Indonesians are used to an overcrowded society; they tend to ignore inadvertent invasions of space. Allowing for personal space is a sign of respect.
* **Rude gestures:** Males do not touch females in public except to shake hands. The head is considered sacred and should not be touched. Looking someone straight in the eyes is considered staring. Point with the thumb, not the index finger, and never beckon with one finger. Approval is sometimes shown with a pat on the shoulder, but American-style backslapping is considered offensive.

Ireland (Irish)

* **Acceptable gestures:** A firm handshake is the common greeting, and eye contact is expected. The Irish are not very comfortable with public displays of affection. They are also uncomfortable with loud, aggressive, and arrogant behavior.
* **Rude gestures:** A reverse "V for victory" gesture is considered obscene.

Israel (Israeli)

* **Acceptable gestures:** Israelis tend to stand close to each other. A warm handshake is customary, and Israelis most often make direct eye contact.
* **Rude gestures:** Moving away from another person when conversing is rude.

Italy (Italians)

* **Acceptable gestures:** Personal relations are highly valued, especially in families. Italians shake hands when meeting and departing. Italians are known for using the most body language of all Europeans. To beckon a person, raise your index finger and make eye contact.
* **Rude gestures:** Flicking the hand underneath the chin is very insulting.

Japan (Japanese)

* **Acceptable gestures:** A handshake is appropriate upon meeting. The Japanese handshake is typically light, with little or no eye contact. Some Japanese bow and shake hands. The bow is a highly regarded greeting to show respect and is appreciated by the Japanese. A slight bow to show courtesy is acceptable. Japanese prefer ample personal space and avoid touching. Nodding is very important when listening to a Japanese person who is learning English. Teachers should nod to show that they are listening and understanding the speaker. In the Japanese culture, silence is a natural and expected form of nonverbal communication. Japanese students do not feel a need to chatter.
* **Rude gestures:** Prolonged eye contact (staring) is considered rude. The Japanese extend their right arm out in front, bending the wrist down and waving fingers to beckon friends. Waving a hand back and forth with palm forward in front of the face means "no" or "I don't know." This is also a polite response to a compliment.

Luxembourg (Luxembourgers)

* **Acceptable gestures:** Luxembourgers are friendly but reserved. Shaking hands with all age levels is considered appropriate. Good friends kiss cheeks, one on each side.
* **Rude gestures:** Do not put your hands in your pockets.

Malaysia (Malaysians)

* **Acceptable gestures:** Shaking hands is common, as is nodding or giving a slight bow. Western women most often greet Malaysian men with a nod of their head and a smile. Affection is not shown in public.

* **Rude gestures:** It is inappropriate to touch anyone on the top of the head (home of the soul), especially a child. The right hand is used to eat, pass things, and touch people. A smile or laugh could mean surprise, anger, shock, embarrassment, or happiness. Single fingers are not used for gesturing. Hitting your fist into a cupped hand is obscene. Hands in pockets signify anger.

Mexico (Mexicans)

* **Acceptable gestures:** Mexicans often "hold" a gesture (a handshake, a squeeze of the arm, a hug) longer than Americans and Canadians do. They generally stand close together when conversing and can consider it rude if the other individual backs away.
* **Rude gestures:** Standing with your hands on your hips can signify anger. It is considered rude to stand with hands in the pockets.

Physical education teachers must remain aware of how their proximity and their gestures might be interpreted—or misinterpreted—by students from other cultures.

Netherlands (Dutch)

*   **Acceptable gestures:** The Dutch are reserved people and seldom touch in public or display anger or extreme exuberance. They value privacy and seldom speak to strangers. The Dutch expect eye contact. They shake hands and say their last name, not "Hello," and also answer the telephone with their last name.

*   **Rude gestures:** It is considered very impolite to shout a greeting or to speak loudly. It is better to wave if you are greeting someone from a distance. Moving the index finger around your ear means you have a telephone call and not "You're crazy." The "crazy" sign is tapping the center of the forehead with the index finger. This gesture is considered very rude.

New Zealand (New Zealanders)

*   **Acceptable gestures:** A handshake with a firm grip and direct eye contact is acceptable.

*   **Rude gestures:** It is considered rude to speak loudly and demonstrate excessive behavior.

Norway (Norwegians)

*   **Acceptable gestures:** Norwegians do little personal touching except between relatives and close friends.

*   **Rude gestures:** It is rude to stand close to a Norwegian, back slap, or put an arm around anyone. Norwegians do not use the phrases "Pleased to meet you" or "How are you?" They consider these surface formalities with no real meaning.

Pakistan (Pakistani)

*   **Acceptable gestures:** The handshake is the acceptable greeting, but the grip should be soft.

*   **Rude gestures:** A closed fist is an obscene gesture.

Paraguay (Paraguayans)

*   **Acceptable gestures:** Men and women always shake hands when greeting even if they have met earlier in the day. Paraguayans kiss twice when meeting friends and family members. Good posture is important. A chin flick (rubbing the hand under the chin) means "I don't know."

*   **Rude gestures:** Never beckon a person from Paraguay with a crooked finger.

Philippines (Filipinos)

*   **Acceptable gestures:** An "eyebrow flash" (i.e., a quick lifting of eyebrows) is a common Filipino greeting. Female friends frequently hold hands in public whereas males do not. If Filipinos don't understand a question, they open their mouths. A quick lifting of the eyebrows signifies recognition and agreement. Laughter may convey pleasure or embarrassment; it is commonly used to relieve tension. "Yes" is signified by a jerk of the head upward. "No" is signified by a jerk of the head down.

*   **Rude gestures:** Staring is considered rude and can be misinterpreted as a challenge. To a Filipino, standing with your hands on your hips means you are angry. Never curl your index finger back and forth (to beckon). This is an insult. To indicate two of something, raise your ring and pinkie fingers. To beckon, extend arm, palm down, moving fingers in a scratching motion. Touch someone's elbow lightly to attract attention. Do not tap on the shoulder.

Portugal (Portuguese)

*   **Acceptable gestures:** When meeting friends, men embrace and pat one another on the back, and women kiss both cheeks. Portuguese do not use many body gestures. Do not be overly demonstrative with hand gestures or body language.

*   **Rude gestures:** Beckon students with the palm of the hand down and the fingers or whole hand waving (as in patting someone on the head).

Russia (Russians)

*   **Acceptable gestures:** Russians stand close when talking and tend to be very demonstrative. Public physical contact is common. Hugs, backslapping, kisses on the cheeks, and other expansive gestures are common among friends or acquaintances and between members of the same sex. Russians stand close when talking.

*   **Rude gestures:** A handshake is always appropriate (but not obligatory) when greeting or leaving, regardless of the relationship. Remove your gloves before shaking hands. Don't shake hands over a threshold (Russian folk belief holds that this action will lead to an argument). Putting your thumb through

your index and middle fingers or making the OK sign is considered a very rude gesture in Russia.

Singapore (Singaporeans)

* **Acceptable gestures:** Handshakes should be firm. Singaporeans may bow slightly as they shake your hand. Many Westerners are generally taller than Singaporeans, so it would be polite to give a small bow.
* **Rude gestures:** Never touch an adult's or a child's head. The head is considered sacred. The foot is considered the lowest part of the body and is thought to be unclean. The foot should never be used to point at someone, and you should never show the bottom of your feet. Raise your hand to get someone's attention. Never signal or point at a person with the forefinger. Do not pound your fist on an open palm; this is considered obscene.

South Korea (Koreans)

* **Acceptable gestures:** Many Koreans consider it a personal violation to be touched by someone who is not a relative or close friend. The bow is the traditional Korean greeting, although it is often accompanied by a handshake. To show respect when shaking hands, support your right forearm with your left hand. Korean women usually nod slightly instead of shaking hands. Koreans frequently bow when departing. Younger people wave (move their arm from side to side). Direct eye contact should be avoided, as it is seen as impolite or even as a challenge. When addressing a Korean, note that Korean names are the opposite of Western names, with the family name followed by the two-part given name.
* **Rude gestures:** Always pass and receive objects with your right hand (supported by the left hand at the wrist or forearm) or with two hands. To beckon an individual, extend the arm, palm down, and move the fingers in a scratching motion. Never point with the index finger.

Spain (Spaniards, Spanish)

* **Acceptable gestures:** Shaking hands is common among all age levels. Men may embrace each other when meeting (friends and family only). Females often kiss each other on the cheek and embrace. Never touch, hug, or back slap a Spaniard unless the person approaches first. Generally, Spaniards stand very close when talking and move their hands while talking.
* **Rude gestures:** Chewing gum while talking is considered rude.

Sweden (Swedes)

* **Acceptable gestures:** Swedes tend to shake hands with everyone, including children, when meeting and parting, but they are generally reserved in their body language. They seldom embrace or touch in public.
* **Rude gestures:** Maintain eye contact at all times while talking with someone.

Switzerland (Swiss)

* **Acceptable gestures:** Handshakes are firm, with eye contact.
* **Rude gestures:** Do not point the index finger to the head. This is an insult. Body language varies from region to region in Switzerland.

Taiwan (Taiwanese)

* **Acceptable gestures:** A nod of the head or a slight bow is considered polite for the first meeting. Handshakes are generally only for males who are friends.
* **Rude gestures:** Do not touch anyone, especially a baby, on top of the head. Affection for the opposite sex is not shown in public. Never use the feet to move an object or to point at an object. Feet are considered dirty. Place the hands in the lap when sitting. Men should not cross their legs but instead place both feet on the floor. Putting an arm around another's shoulder, winking, and pointing with your index finger are all considered rude gestures. Point with an open hand. Palm facing outward in front of the face and moving back and forth means "no."

Thailand (Thai)

* **Acceptable gestures:** The Thai greet each other with the "wai" (why). Foreigners are not expected to initiate the wai gesture, but it is an insult not to return the wai. To give the wai, people place the palms of their hands together, with their fingers extended at chest level close to their body, and bow slightly. The higher the hands are placed, the more respect is shown. Subordinates might

raise their fingers as high as their nose, but the tips of the fingers should never be above eye level. A wai can mean "Hello," "Thank you," "I'm sorry," or "Goodbye." The Thai say "Where are you going?" rather than "Hello." A polite response is "Just down the street."

* **Rude gestures:** To bump, hit, rub, or touch a student's head is considered very rude.

Turkey (Turks)

* **Acceptable gestures:** Turks generally have a small area of personal space and may stand closer than most foreigners are used to standing. It is common for Turkish men and women to cheek kiss one another when meeting and parting. "Yes" is a slight downward nod of the head. "No" is a slight upward nod of the head accompanied by a quick sucking sound through the two front teeth (like "tsk").

* **Rude gestures:** Never point the sole of the foot toward a person. Turks often avoid looking into your eyes in a display of humble behavior. In Turkey, putting your thumb between the first two fingers is the equivalent to raising your middle finger in the United States. The OK sign in Turkey is viewed as a reference to homosexuality and is offensive.

United Kingdom

* **Acceptable gestures:** Four countries make up the United Kingdom of Great Britain and Northern Ireland: England, Scotland, Wales, and Northern Ireland. In England, politeness, reserve, and restraint are admired. The English are courteous, unassuming, unabrasive, and very proud of their long and rich history. Scots are passionate about their country and are free of class consciousness and social elitism, except in religion. Scots have a keen, subtle sense of humor and value generosity. Wales has its own language, literature, and traditions. The Welsh love to sing and talk and spend much of their free time with their families. The British like a certain amount of personal space, and they are not back slappers or touchers and seldom display affection in public.

* **Rude gestures:** Staring is considered rude in the United Kingdom. Do not stand too close to another person or put your arm around someone's shoulder. Another rude gesture is the reverse "V for victory" sign made with the palm toward the body.

Uruguay (Uruguayans)

* **Acceptable gestures:** Greetings are warm and are accompanied by a firm handshake. Friends kiss once on the right cheek when meeting. Uruguayans stand very close when conversing, both socially and in business. People touch shoulders and hold arms while they talk to each other.

* **Rude gestures:** The North American OK sign is extremely rude. You may see people brush the backs of their hands under their chins to signal "I don't know."

Venezuela (Venezuelans)

* **Acceptable gestures:** Greetings are warm and friendly. Handshakes are common among strangers, and Venezuelans stand very close when speaking. Maintain eye contact when talking.

* **Rude gestures:** Seating posture is important. Try to keep both feet on the floor, and avoid slouching. Casual touching is common among males. The North American OK sign is extremely rude.

Vietnam (Vietnamese)

* **Acceptable gestures:** The Vietnamese generally shake hands both when greeting and when saying good-bye. Vietnamese women are more inclined to bow their head slightly than to shake hands. Men and women do not show affection in public, but members of the same sex may hold hands while walking.

* **Rude gestures:** Touching children on the head is done only by close relatives like parents and grandparents.

PRACTICE 4:
Address the Needs of English Language Learners

The goal of many physical education teachers is to offer their students a variety of instructional strategies, including the more advanced teaching styles such as the constructivist approach. The constructivist approach requires the student to come up with the most accurate or correct physical or verbal response to a series of well-developed questions based on prior knowledge. However, this aspiration is less than realistic when a student's understanding of English is limited or even non-existent. Since many urban home settings do not provide a language-rich environment, physical education teachers may find themselves in classes with a large population of English language learners (ELL). These teachers can assist students by making greater use of a teacher-directed style, using a variety of cognates (as explained on p. 18) and devising simple systems of rotation, among other techniques.

Probably the most widely used teacher-directed approach stems from Mosston and Ashworth's (2002) command style of teaching. This instructional strategy provides a basic structure for ELL students to follow beginning when the student is prompted to imitate the teacher with initial warm-up stretches. Second, the ELL student develops an image of the key elements of the movement

skill or advanced sport skill when the teacher (or a capable student) physically demonstrates the task. The teacher's introductory physical demonstration and subsequent visual modeling for the ELL student to imitate are critical. The ELL student's sport skill vocabulary is greatly expanded when the teacher repeats the instructional cues several times, and the style's basic stop and go signals can help to decrease students' frustration. Third, the style is effective even with limited equipment and space; and fourth, the quick pace of the lesson increases the likelihood that the ELL student will remain on task for a higher percentage of the lesson.

Mosston and Ashworth's (2002) practice style is also effective when one is working with ELL students in urban settings. The teacher starts with a demonstration and brief description of what is to be achieved. The demonstration may use a student to model the skill or even a visual aid. Gymnastics movements and other isolated skill techniques can

Overcrowding is a serious problem in many large urban schools that are forced to look for creative ways to serve their students adequately.

be taught through a series of pictures. Illustrations depicting playing positions, rule infractions, and basic offense and defense strategies also help to clarify directions and correct misunderstandings. Teachers can also reinforce the names of sport skills by posting them on a bulletin board or writing them on poster board for display on the wall. This word wall with subject-specific vocabulary words should be highly visible to the students. This step is followed by students practicing the skill on their own, with a partner, or with a group as the physical education teacher observes their performance and offers feedback. This teaching style is popular in urban settings perhaps because of its similarity to the way most urban teachers coach a sport or have students practice sport skills.

For example, an urban coach who is showing a team a particular basketball shot normally explains the fundamental mechanics of the shot and identifies when and why it is used. This is followed by one or more demonstrations of the skill, again emphasizing its key elements. The players are then given time to practice by themselves or with a partner. The coach walks around making corrections, repeatedly demonstrating when necessary, and providing encouragement. At the end of a typical practice session emphasizing cues and providing encouragement, the coach asks the players to identify the key points before going on to the next practice session. This basic format for introducing new sport skills can be successfully used in most urban settings with ELL students. Advocates of the practice style believe that non-English-speaking students may benefit most from physical education teachers who "talk less–move more" by circulating throughout the gymnasium and serving as a model for the students to imitate.

Multiple Languages

In New York City, 40 percent of students in the schools live in households where a language other than English is spoken, and one-third were born in another country. Thus, New York City's Department of Education translates report cards into eight languages: Spanish, Chinese, Urdu, Russian, Bengali, Haitian Creole, Korean, and Arabic.

Use Cognates

Urban teachers can also increase their likelihood of success when teaching ELL students by making use of cognates. Cognates are words in different languages that have the same linguistic derivation and thus are similar. Knowledge of these words assists the physical education teacher who has resorted to using only hand signals and demonstrations. For example, Spanish has easy-to-remember words for recreation *(recreación)*, to move forward *(avanzar)*, purpose *(propósito)*, to join *(juntar)*, and protection *(protección)*. Examples in Italian include *gli sport* (sport), *associate* (partner), *guardare* (guard), *grupo* (group), and *passeggero* (passenger). Words from French include *le sport* (sport), *finir* (finish), *les raquettes* (paddles), *signal* (signal), *marcher* (walk), and *porter* (carry). It is also important to note that many words depicting shapes and forms are very similar in numerous languages and may be used to structure practice formations. Examples include *circle* (English), *el círculo* (Spanish), *il cerchio* (Italian), and *le cercle* (French). Likewise, students can be asked to practice skills in triangular formations, for example *el triángulo* (Spanish), *triangolo* (Italian), and *le triangle* (French). The names of particular sports are also very similar among languages (table 1.3).

Find Similarities in Sports

In addition to using cognates, teachers can decrease many of the difficulties associated with introducing unfamiliar activities to ELL students by identifying similarities between North American activities and activities from the student's native country. For example, the North American activities of horseshoes and lawn darts can be compared to the Italian game of bocce, or boules, as it is called in France. The striking and base running skills emphasized in softball and stickball resemble fundamental techniques in cricket. Similarities also exist in strategies and rules. Whenever possible, it is advisable to introduce an activity by pointing out the similarity of its rules or strategies to those of a well-known sport (e.g., "Unihoc uses many of the same strategies, rules, and skills as ice hockey or field hockey"). The identification of these similarities help students transfer previously learned skills to new activities when language is a barrier.

Table 1.3 Examples of Name Similarities in Sport

United States	Spain	Italy	France
Cycling	el ciclismo	il ciclismo	le cyclisme
Baseball	el béisbol	il baseball	le base-ball
Skiing	el esquí	lo sci	le ski
Tennis	el tenis	il tennis	le tennis
Judo	el judo	il judo	le judo
Gymnastics	la gymnasia	la ginnastica	la gymnastique

Devise Simple Systems of Rotation

Instructing individuals to perform even the most basic movement rotation (e.g., moving from station to station) can result in a chaotic situation when language differences exist. One technique to overcome grouping and rotational problems involves using colors as a form of student identification. To begin, each student selects a small piece of colored construction paper from a hat that contains three or four different colors, depending on the number of desired groups. Following the selection, teacher assistants are assigned individually to supervise a specific color group. These individuals identify themselves to the students by waving their colored paper in the air and motioning to students with the same color to follow them to a designated area for instruction.

Communication Strategies With ELL Students

When speaking one-on-one to a newly identified ELL student, some teachers are at a loss as to how best to proceed. Unfortunately, the physical education teacher is often the last teacher to receive a completed written report with specific background information on the new student. This situation can continue for several class periods. The following series of communication strategies can help teachers with speaking one-on-one to an ELL student.

* Decide ahead of time what specific key points must be communicated and focus only on these.
* Convey a sequence that the student is to follow (e.g., "First you . . . and then second you . . . ," or "1, 2, and now 3").
* Use visuals if possible or even a written explanation in the student's native language.

* Use simple words to convey thoughts.
* Watch for information overload in the student's facial expression.
* Watch for the nonverbal cues signaling a lack of understanding (e.g., shaking the head).
* Use consistent terminology for communication and sports.
* Avoid mumbling or slurring words and speak clearly and slowly, since hearing English spoken too quickly causes the most anxiety in ELL students, even when they already know the words. They are still using their internal translator, which takes time.
* Emphasize or repeat the key words and skills at least three times.
* Avoid asking "Do you understand?"
* Do not yell. Raising your voice level will not help a student understand the directions more effectively.
* Work to elicit trust between students having difficulties interacting within large groups.
* Avoid intimidating phrases (e.g., "You must," "You should," or "I require").
* Convey high expectations for student success and give verbal reinforcement to both genders.
* Keep in mind that you can avoid initial communication problems altogether when you encourage immediate participation by beginning lessons with equipment that particular (teacher-led) movement skills are naturally associated with (e.g., Frisbees, jump ropes, or stretch bands). Using objects that naturally afford a specific movement alleviates early language problems.
* Remember: All teachers should aid students in the mastery of Standard American English.

PRACTICE 5:
Use Nondiscriminatory Selection Techniques, International Skill Practice Formations, and Urban Ways to Start a Game

Interpersonal relationships are more likely to develop when individuals are encouraged to work with different partners throughout the school year. The following partner selection techniques facilitate this process and help students identify basic similarities and interests. Whenever possible, repeat these techniques throughout the lesson so that students are not always working with the same people. Avoid using selection techniques that focus only on hair or eye color since people from many cultures have similar features as a characteristic of their ethnic background.

Individuals should be encouraged to work with a partner based on these commonalities:

* The same birthday season (fall, winter, spring, summer) or the same birth month
* The same height, same arm length, or same shoe size
* The same first initial in the first name or the last name
* The same number of vowels in the last name
* The same number of letters in the first name or the last name
* The same number of brothers or same number of sisters
* Ability to speak two languages
* Participation in the same number of sports even if they are not the same sports

When selecting groups, teachers should avoid having captains responsible for dividing their peers into teams. This can lead to disagreements and also lower the self-image of those chosen last. One alternative to this technique involves asking students to form a side-by-side line. On the teacher's signal (1-2-3), have the students close their eyes and respond to one of the following:

* Jump either one step forward or one step backward.
* Either stretch the body upward or stoop downward.
* Create a grip with either the right hand or the left hand.

* Either make an X with your arms in front of your body or make an O with your arms stretched above your head.
* Pretend to catch a ground ball or a fly ball.
* Pretend to shoot a basketball or dribble a basketball.

In the event that the outcome is not even, the teacher asks the students from the larger group to repeat until the groups are equal in number.

Teachers can also cut small strips of construction paper and have the student pull a colored strip from a hat or envelope. Or, students can be asked to write a number on a small piece of paper, and the teacher can divide the group according to the odd or even numbers. Students can also be divided according to birthdays in the months of January through June or the months of July through December. In all cases, alternative grouping techniques increase the likelihood that students will experience a more friendly form of competition and will participate in different groups throughout the year.

Group Selection Techniques From Different Countries

Students from the United States are very intrigued when they are given the opportunity to experience novel ways of dividing groups. These techniques can be used when a class of students is divided into practice groups or when they are asked to challenge another group during class.

Chinese Method

The Chinese have a unique technique for selecting teams. To begin, all students stand in a circle with their hands flat on their chests. On the teacher's count of three, each student puts one hand into the circle, either palm up or down. Palm up is called white, and palm down represents black. If the outcome is not even, the teacher asks the players from the larger group to repeat the action until the teams are equal in number. If the end result is one person representing the odd number, that player selects which team he would like to join.

Roman Method

Many Italian coaches and physical education teachers divide their groups into two teams by first asking all students to form one long line of players facing forward (figure 1.1a). The teacher or coach walks down to the middle of the line and uses her hand to "slice" the line (figure 1.1b).

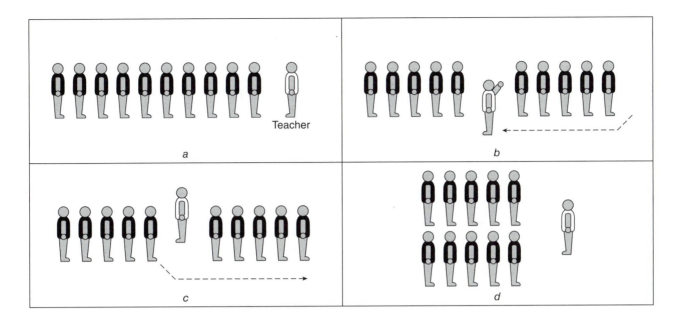

Figure 1.1   The Roman group selection method.

The first player (where the slice occurred) walks or "marches" up to the front, followed by all the remaining players (figure 1.1c). The group is now two equal teams (figure 1.1d).

Brazilian Method

Many Brazilian coaches and physical activity teachers use a very quick and effective technique to divide a large group into two teams. To begin, the teacher asks all players to form a long line with each player standing behind another (figure 1.2a). The teacher stands at the front of the line and begins to "walk into" the line of players while also using one hand to signal which side a student should quickly step to so that the teacher can pass (figure 1.2b). At the end of the walk, the line of players has been divided into two groups (figure 1.2c).

Starting a Game the Urban Way

There are many ways to begin a game. The first move in a game often gives a player or a team an advantage over the opponent. Many methods of deciding who will have the first move rely on luck or chance and are therefore fair. The following techniques are just a few that were commonly used on city streets before there were referees or officials to begin recreational play.

Coin Flip

One person, either a student or another peer or the teacher, makes a fist and places a coin (with a head and a tail) on the thumbnail. The coin is flipped with a sharp flick of the thumb. It will spin in the air and can be caught or allowed to hit the ground. If the coin is caught, it should be caught with one hand and slapped on the back of the free hand. Before the coin is revealed, the players are asked, "Heads or tails?" The student who guesses correctly has the privilege of going first or passing to the other team. If the coin is allowed to hit the ground, the decision on heads or tails is made while the coin is still in the air.

Which Hand?

One student holds a coin in one hand and hides his hands behind his back. He can change the hand that holds the coin or keep it in the same hand. He then brings the two clenched fists out in front, and his opponent must guess which hand is holding the coin. If the opponent guesses correctly, he has the first move. If not, the first move belongs to the student who hid the coin.

Last Straw or Stick

A group of sticks or a bunch of straws is emptied onto a table or any flat surface. Two students take turns picking up one item at a time. The student who is left with the last item to pick up begins the game.

Odds and Evens

Two students stand with one hand clenched in a fist behind their backs. One player calls "Odds"

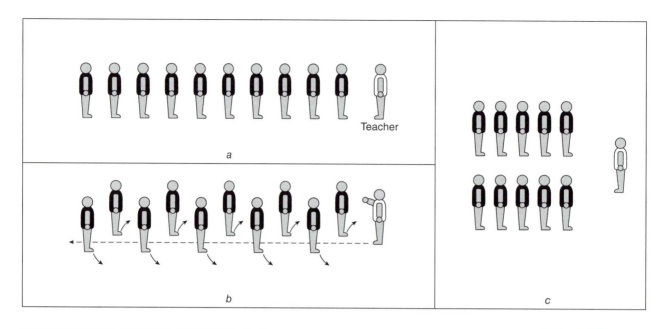

Figure 1.2   The Brazilian group selection method.

People have used the "hands on the bat" technique of choosing who goes first for years.

number zero. The sum of the combined fingers will be either an odd or an even number. The student who called the correct answer begins the game. One round or the best of three rounds can be played. This is a variation of the Japanese game called Jankepon.

Hands on the Bat

Two students stand and face each other. One student tosses a baseball bat to the other, who catches it with one hand near the bottom end. The two players take turns grabbing the bat as their hands move along its length. The sides of their hands must touch as they move. This process continues until there is just enough room at the top for one full hand. The student who is the last to grab the bat begins the game.

Rock, Paper, and Scissors

This method involves three symbols instead of the typical "odds and evens." Each symbol has an advantage and a disadvantage: Rock (clenched fist) breaks scissors; scissors (two fingers spread apart) cut paper; paper (open palm) covers rock. Rock beats scissors but loses to paper; scissors beats paper but loses to rock; and paper beats rock but loses to scissors. Students chant, "Rock, paper, scissors, shoot" and show their symbol on the word *shoot*.

and the other player calls "Evens." Then they say, "One, two, three, shoot" in unison and stick out either one or two fingers. Players can also reveal up to five fingers or keep a closed fist for the

International Practice Formations

The following formations have a long history of existence in countries throughout the world. They are suggested as a means for the teacher to have all students practice a throwing, catching, or kicking skill to enhance their performance during game play. They are also extremely useful when the teacher's lack of equipment necessitates larger group practice situations.

Key
- - - - - - → Movement
——————→ Skill (e.g., throw, catch, kick)

Line and Leader (Germany)

Student moves to the end of the line after the skill (e.g., throw) is performed. The leader remains stationary.

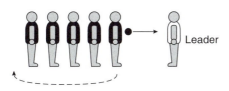

Line and Leader Variation (Denmark)

All students and the leader remain stationary. Leader throws to first student, who throws back to the leader.

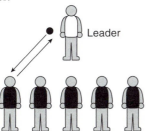

Double Lines (Chile)

Students throw to the end of the line, and the last player runs to the first position. All players advance to the next space.

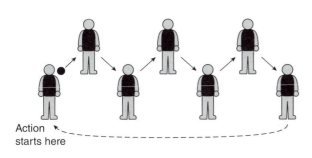

Star (United States)

Students throw in a star formation.

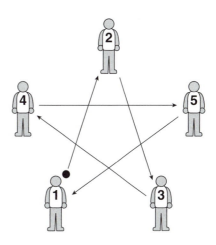

Circle and Leader (Colombia)

All students remain stationary. After the leader throws to all students, he switches places with a circle player.

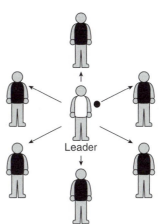

Advanced Triple Star (Israel)

Student throws to the next numbered player and moves as quickly as possible to the end of the line that the student had just thrown to in the formation.

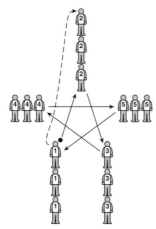

Basic Shuttle (Argentina)

Student moves to the end of his line after the throw.

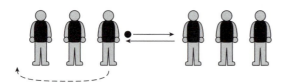

Advanced Shuttle (Canada)

Student performs the throw and moves to the end of the opposite line.

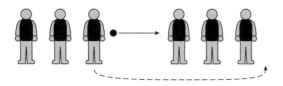

Triangle (Scotland)

Students throw in a triangle formation.

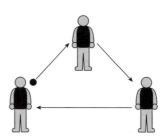

Fast Pass Trio (Uruguay)

Student passes in a triangle formation and quickly moves to the end of her line after the throw.

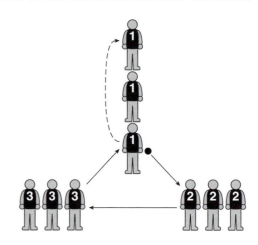

Advanced Shuttle (Australia)

This shuttle requires large-group cooperation. To begin, student 1 throws at an angle to student 2 in the opposite line. Student 1 immediately moves to the end of his line. Student 2 then throws at an angle back to student 1's line and moves to the end of his own line. After the students have practiced this throwing formation, add a second ball for a greater challenge.

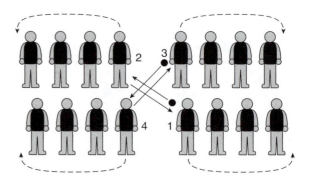

PRACTICE 6:
Enhance the Learning Environment With Themed Bulletin Boards and Greetings

Nowhere is the element of participation more in question than in a class of 40 to 100 middle or high school students. The urban teacher of large classes needs ongoing physical and emotional stamina and a commitment to inclusion. Teachers so committed can start by providing an appealing learning environment. Attractive bulletin boards, wall murals, and sport photographs, as well as drawings, charts, posters, and cultural information relating to sport, send the message that physical education is an important part of everyone's middle or high school experience regardless of size, gender, culture, or physical ability. Bulletin board messages also convey that the gymnasium is a safe place for learning, both physically and socially.

The following are urban-themed bulletin board messages in three categories that may be especially significant to students reared in low socioeconomic settings: overcoming failure, striving to achieve more, and offering a helping hand.

Overcoming Failure

* Persistent people begin and succeed where others fail.
* It is not how much we have, but how much we enjoy!
* You have only failed when you have failed to try!
* There are no problems, only solutions!
* Nobody can acquire honor by doing what is wrong.
* You can't win today on what you did in the last race.
* When you make a mistake, be the first to admit it.
* Speaking without thinking is like shooting without aiming.
* Visualize it.
* Make it happen!
* Meet your problems with decision.
* The best way out of a difficulty is through it.
* Believe in yourself.

* The greatest thing in the world is not so much where we are, but the direction we are moving in.
* It is a funny thing about life; if you refuse to accept anything but the best, you very often get it.
* Destiny is not a matter of chance; it is a matter of choice.
* Failure is not the worst thing in the world. The very worst is not to try.
* People can alter their lives by altering their attitudes.
* Trouble is usually produced by those who produce nothing else.
* Nature gives talent, but it is up to the person to make it work.
* Weak people wait for opportunities; strong people make them.
* Anger is only one letter short of danger.
* Opportunities are useless unless used.
* Failure is no more a permanent condition than is success.

Striving to Achieve More

* Anything is within your reach!
* The past can teach you; the present can test you; the future can reward you.
* Enjoy learning new things, reading new books, thinking new thoughts!
* People are divided into three groups: those who make things happen, those who watch things happen, and those who wonder what happened!
* Most problems are really the absence of ideas!
* The past is my heritage, the present is my responsibility, the future is my challenge!
* Forget the misgivings in your past and move on to greater achievements in the future!
* Aim at nothing and you'll hit it.
* Leadership is accepting responsibility.
* Winners are workers.
* Hustle is the only indispensible quality of a champion.
* The number of talents we have is less important than using them.
* Genius is 1 percent inspiration and 99 percent perspiration.

* Give the game the best you have and the best will come back to you.
* The difference between a true athlete and an amateur is desire.
* The difference between the impossible and the possible lies in a person's determination.
* Do not let what you cannot do interfere with what you can do.
* Don't wait for your ship to come in; swim out to it.
* You may not have been responsible for your heritage, but you are responsible for your future.
* Real leaders are ordinary people with extraordinary determination.
* People with goals succeed because they know where they're going.
* The difference between a successful person and others is not a lack of strength, not a lack of knowledge, but rather a lack of will.
* Life is a mirror—if you frown at it, it frowns back; if you smile, it returns the greeting.
* Patience is the ability to hold your tongue when you are tempted to lose your cool.
* Physical fitness—a matter of pride in one's self.
* The largest room in the world is the room for improvement.
* Give 100 percent all of the time.
* Success is the result of hard work and honest effort.

Offering a Helping Hand

* We share the earth!
* Be just as enthusiastic about the success of others as you are about your own!
* To be happy you must forget yourself!
* Accept life's challenges with a friend!
* It is more important to be human than to be important!
* Discover your interests, potentials, and talents with a friend!
* We're all in this together!
* It is amazing how much can be accomplished if no one cares who gets the credit!
* No act of kindness, no matter how small, is ever wasted!
* The more honor and respect among your teammates, the greater the team.

* Sportsmanship is like dirt—it rubs off.
* The best place to find a helping hand is at the end of your arm.
* Don't tell me how good you are—let me find it out.
* Leadership is based on inspiration, not domination; on cooperation, not intimidation.
* What happens to us is important; our response to what happens to us is vital.
* The team that won't be beaten can't be beaten.
* Character is measured by conduct.
* The person who is wrapped up in him- or herself makes a very small package.
* Success means to appreciate the best in others and acknowledge shortcomings in ourselves.

Teachers can also increase the students' interest if they identify the sizes of various balls used in sport participation by placing the information on a bulletin board or conveying the information as part of the lesson introduction (table 1.4). Many students are amused to learn that the length of a football in the National Football League, the National Collegiate Athletic Association, and high school is 11.25 inches and that it originated from the original English rugby ball of 12 inches, hence the name "football."

Another bulletin board theme that tends to arouse students' curiosity about sports from other countries involves identifying the sports according to alphabet letters. When the listing is made available, recently immigrated students are pleased to see their favorite sport displayed. Students can also be encouraged to add to the list.

A-to-Z Sport Awareness Throughout the World

A. Australian football, archery, aquatics
B. badminton, ballet, baseball, basketball, bowling, boxing, biathlon, bobsleigh, bocce, bodybuilding
C. cricket, cycling, canoe, curling, climbing, cheerleading, chess, cross-country running
D. diving, dancing, downhill skiing, decathlon
E. equestrian
F. footy, football, fencing, floor hockey
G. Gaelic football, gymnastics, golf
H. horse racing, hockey, high jump, handball, hang gliding, horseshoes

Table 1.4 Diameter of Sporting Balls From Around the World

Sport	Measurement (inches)	Measurement (centimeters)
Table tennis	1.57	4
Squash	1.57	4
Golf	1.68	4.3
Handball	2	5
Jai alai	2	5
Pool (British)	2	5
Billiards (American)	2.25	5.7
Paddle tennis	2.5	6.4
Lacrosse	2.5	6.4
Tennis	2.7	6.9
Field hockey	2.81	7.1
Cricket	2.87	7.3
Baseball	2.9	7.4
Polo (outdoor)	3.25	8.3
Softball (10 and under)	3.5	8.9
Croquet	3.625	9.2
Softball (12 to college)	3.8	9.7
Bocce	4.3	10.9
Water polo (women's)	8.44	21.4
Volleyball*	8.5	21.6
Bowling	between 8.5 and 8.595	between 21.6 and 21.8
Soccer	8.65	22
Footy	8.9	22.6
Water polo (men's)	8.92	22.7
Basketball (women's)	9.07	23
Gaelic football (Irish)	9.2	23.4
Basketball (men's)	9.39	23.9
Football	11.25	28.6
Rugby	12	30.5
Medicine ball (traditional)	roughly 14 (diameter of the shoulders)	roughly 35.6

*A tether ball is roughly the same size as a volleyball.

I. ice hockey, ice skating, in-line skating

J. judo

K. karate, kayaking

L. lawn bowls, long jump, luge, lacrosse

M. motor bike racing, mountain bike racing, modern pentathlon

N. netball, newcomb, national basketball, national rugby

O. orienteering

P. pole vault, Paralympics, Ping-Pong, parachuting, paddleball, powerlifting

Q. quoits

R. riflery, rugby, running, rowing, roller skating, rock climbing

S. skating, soccer, squash, swimming, sailing, shooting, skiing, surfing, softball, sumo, shot put, skateboarding, scuba diving, snowshoeing, synchronized swimming, speed skating, snow boarding

T. tennis, triple jump, table tennis, taekwondo, triathlon, tug-of-war, tenpins, track and field, tchoukball

U. underwater polo, unihoc

V. volleyball

W. winter sports, wrestling, water polo, weightlifting, water skiing, wind surfing

X. xtreme sports

Y. yoga

Z. Z-ball

Another bulletin board idea is to show how to say hello in various languages (table 1.5). This theme not only is useful to a teacher addressing a new student from a foreign country but also seems to intrigue students. For example, many U.S. students have immigrant grandparents who speak their native language fluently, and a list such as this indicates simple greetings from their own heritage.

Table 1.5   Conveying Hello in Different Languages

Language	"Hello"	Pronunciation
Arabic	Al Salaam a'alaykum	Ahl sah-LAHM ah ah-LAY-koom
Armenian	Barev	Bar-ev
Bulgarian	Zdraveite	ZZ-DRA-veyt
Cantonese	Nei hou	Nay hoe
Cherokee	O si yo	Oh-see-YOH
Croatian	Bok	BOHk
Czech	Dobry den	DO-bry den
Danish	Goddag	Go dah
Dutch	Hallo	Hal-low
Estonian	Tere	TER-e
Finnish	Terve	TER-vey
French	Bonjour	Bohn-ZHOOR
German	Guten Tag	GOOT-en tahk
Greek	Kalimera	Kah-lee-MEH-rah

Table 1.5 *(continued)*

Language	"Hello"	Pronunciation
Hebrew	Shalom	Sha-LOHM
Hindi	Namaste	Nah-mah-STAY
Hungarian	Szia	ZEE-yah
Icelandic	Hallo	Hal-lo
Indonesian	Assalamu alai kum	Ahl sah-LAHM ah-LAY-koom
Italian	Buon giorno	Bwohn JOR-noh
Japanese	Konnichiwa	Kon-NEE-chee wah
Korean	Annyong ha shimnikka	An-YOH HASH-im-ni-kah
Lithuanian	Labas	Lah-bahs
Mandarin	Ni Hao	Knee how
Mayan	Ba'ax ka wa'alik	BAH-ah shko-WAH al-LEEK
Mohawk	Sekoh	SHE-goh
Navajo	Ya at eeh	YAH-AHT-AY
Norwegian	God dag	Goo-dagh
Persian	Selam	She-lam
Polish	Czesc	Chesht
Portuguese	Oi	Oy
Romanian	Buna ziua	BOO-nuh ZEE-wa
Russian	Zdraustvuite	ZzDRAST-voyt-yah
Samoan	Talofa lava	Tah-lo-fa la-va
Serbian	Zdravo	ZDRAH-vo
Slovak	Dobry den	Dobree den
Slovenian	Zdravo	ZDRAD-vo
Spanish	Hola	OH-la
Swahili	Jambo	JAM-bo
Swedish	God dag	Goo dag
Turkish	Merhaba	MER-ha-ba
Ukranian	Pryvit	Pri-veet
Ute	Mique	Mak
Vietnamese	Xin chao	Seen chow
Welsh	Bore da	BOY-ray DAH

SUMMARY

Clearly, implementing culturally responsive teaching practices in physical education at the middle and high school level means being aware of diversity issues to plan everyday physical education lessons. Effective teachers not only are aware of the continuous demographic changes taking place in their school but also respond to the cultural needs of students by recognizing individual characteristics reflecting race, ethnicity, country of origin, and intercultural differences in gestures and body language. An effective teacher is prepared to address the needs of ELL students, uses nondiscriminatory partner and group selection techniques, acquaints the students with inter-national skill practice formations, and enhances the learning environment with little-known sport-related facts and cultural greetings.

Culturally responsive teaching practices encourage all students to participate throughout the lesson or at least during some part of it. However, people should not be forced to participate or manipulated into participation. Instead, play should begin without the individual who is resistant. At some point in the activity, the teacher should ask a student with demonstrated enthusiasm to approach the reluctant individual and suggest that they change roles, thereby allowing a natural form of substitution. In most cases, peer reinforcement works well in all cultures.

URBAN PHYSICAL EDUCATION TEACHERS AS LEADERS

Over the years, educational philosophers have pondered the proverbial question "Are exceptional teachers made or born?" While this issue will continue to be debated, school administrators agree that effective teachers hold and communicate high expectations for their students, and that they believe in themselves and their abilities to convey a strong vision and standard for success. In addition, successful urban teachers use nonverbal messages and overt behaviors, stemming from both their teacher training and their persona, to convey this belief. This combination of beliefs and overt behavior is known as a teacher's professional demeanor. A well-established professional demeanor decreases the likelihood of disruptive, disrespectful, and delinquent student behavior that occurs when students feel that their teacher's classroom presence is shaky or lacking. It also helps experienced urban teachers minimize the myriad distractions that steal energy from their content delivery.

Although in the past the concept has not received great emphasis, in the physical education profession many urban school leaders and administrators (and the authors of this resource) strongly believe that no amount of teacher training alone can guarantee an effective lesson unless the urban teacher has established a professional demeanor. A physical education teacher's demeanor is his or her outward behavior toward the students. On one end of the continuum, some teachers cheer their students' efforts on, show obvious friendliness, and have a pleasing or pleasant demeanor. Others put their students at ease with their calm or reassuring demeanor, and teachers with soft voices and modest gestures tend to have a gentle demeanor. On the opposite end, teachers who appear inflexible or rigid are often seen as having a cool or cold demeanor. Some may appear standoffish and have a sober demeanor, whereas a more dignified or distinguished demeanor might characterize teachers who emphasize leadership qualities.

Teachers in general have the task of demonstrating a professional demeanor that includes exhibiting behaviors and actions such as smiling, appearing supportive and attentive, and praising their students' efforts. However, one of the main responsibilities of urban teachers is to maintain their professional demeanor on a daily basis despite frequent triggers that are likely to rattle a teacher's positive attitude. The word *trigger* is used in urban schools to refer to a difficult student behavior. These behaviors include use of profanity, abusive language, or lewd gestures. Identifying likely triggers can help urban physical education teachers determine how far they can drift from their preferred teacher demeanor while delivering content and still be at ease when a student's behavior is disruptive.

Likewise, identifying elements of one's preferred professional demeanor before employment could assist an individual whose teaching appointment does not allow for a long induction period before working with large class sizes. The Center for Research on the Education of Students Placed at Risk (Ellison et al. 2000) found that a teacher's demeanor was a major factor in setting the tone for the classroom on any given day. Factors that were especially important to the teacher's success included his degree of approachability, his manner of speaking, and his tolerance for movement or noise.

EXAMINING ONE'S TEACHING DEMEANOR

Given the alarming fact that one-third of all new teachers in the United States leave the profession within five years (Education Commission of the States 2000), it is advantageous to place importance on developing and strengthening the teacher's appropriate outward behaviors, actions, and verbal responses to complex situations, as opposed to focusing only on teaching dispositions. Teaching disposition denotes a teacher's willingness to perform an action or adopt an attitude regarding an issue. However, dispositions do not necessarily help a teacher maintain an orderly, purposeful class. Therefore, most teachers can benefit by completing a brief self-analysis to identify elements of their desired teaching demeanor or to learn how to strengthen their existing teacher presence.

Preservice teachers should answer the questions in figure 2.1, and practicing or experienced teachers should answer the questions in figure 2.2. In each case, it is most helpful to write the responses on paper to help with answering the last composite question. All questions are intended

to lay a foundation for developing or expanding one's professional demeanor. Furthermore, self-analysis is a first step in identifying, selecting, and implementing elements of effective instruction that is well presented and is also sensitive to the students' diverse learning needs.

It is also important to remember that any failures teachers experience in an urban school setting are not necessarily attributable to the dynamics existing in the school's community or the surrounding environment, but may be attributable to the physical education teacher's inability to analyze those dynamics and provide ways to correct the situation in the gymnasium. This notion is very difficult for most new teachers to acknowledge unless they have observed urban colleagues who have obvious teacher presence and effectively make the most of every class session. Thus it is important for physical education teachers to have established their preferred professional demeanor during the early induction years and to continually demonstrate an ongoing level of confidence and presence. Early success could decrease the urban teacher's urge to transfer to smaller schools and possibly increase the number of experienced mentors for future professionals.

One way to develop or sustain a professional teaching demeanor is to explore personal qualities such as gravitas that coincide with the desire for self-control over one's emotions, poise under pressure, and ongoing determination. Gravitas originated from an ancient Roman virtue meaning "a sense of dignity, seriousness, and continued duty for the task at hand" (NovaRoma.org). When applying this quality to their professional demeanor, urban physical education teachers make a conscious effort to dress the part, act the part, and

Professional Demeanor Behaviors for Urban Physical Education Settings

Calm, patient, confident, enduring	versus	Anxious
Persistent, independent	versus	Indecisive
Dependable, reliable	versus	Absentminded
Flexible, versatile, optimistic	versus	Pessimistic
Ambitious, outgoing, energetic	versus	Timid
Poised, polite, tactful, tolerant, diplomatic	versus	Flustered
Having gravitas, determination	versus	Hesitant

Developing a Professional Demeanor

1. What five words would your peers and family members use to describe your personality? Are you comfortable with what they would say? Which qualities might assist your interactions with future students? _____

    _____

2. Identify five words that people you have worked with in the past, or are working with now, would use to describe your work demeanor. Which qualities might assist your interactions with future students or might be useful to you in future physical education lessons? _____

    _____

    _____

3. Have you seen specific teaching behaviors that you would like to emulate? If so, describe them. _____

    _____

    _____

4. Would you describe yourself as a confident person? When are you the most confident? _____

    _____

5. Do you prefer to make changes gradually or as quickly as possible? _____

    _____

6. Do you enjoy multitasking and performing several functions simultaneously?

    _____

7. Do you find it easy to laugh at yourself or admit your mistakes? _____

    _____

8. Can you see yourself spending a good part of every lesson encouraging and nurturing students as well as teaching them? _____

    _____

9. To what extent are you willing to be held accountable for problems and issues in your future classes that are not completely under your control? _____

    _____

    _____

10. Given your responses to questions 1 through 9 and the list of teacher behaviors on page 32, write one sentence that emphasizes the behaviors you would like to incorporate into your future teaching demeanor. _____

    _____

    _____

Figure 2.1 Questions for preservice teachers.

From R.L Clements and A. Meltzer Rady, 2012, *Urban physical education: Instructional practices and cultural activities* (Champaign, IL: Human Kinetics).

Strengthening a Professional Demeanor

1. How would you describe your preferred verbal communication with your students? What changes, if any, would you like to make?_____

_____

2. How important is it to you to be in charge or command of your classes?

_____

3. How successful would your students be at discovering the best way to perform a skill or concept on their own? Does your professional demeanor contribute to their response?

   _____ Very successful

   _____ Somewhat successful

   _____ Not at all successful (disaster)

4. Which of the following forms of nonverbal communication do you rely on in your teaching?

   _____ Body motion (circulating around the gym)

   _____ Touching behavior such as handshakes, high fives, pats on the back

   _____ Body positioning (the amount of personal space you leave between yourself and a student)

   _____ Use of eye contact

   _____ Use of facial expressions

   _____ A variety of hand gestures (raising your fist upward as a way of saying "good job")

5. Have you found some forms of teacher nonverbal communication more effective than others while performing any of the following activities? Write Y or N on each line.

   _____ Warm-up stretches

   _____ Introducing the movement or advanced sport skill

   _____ Facilitating the student's level of physical activity

   _____ Practicing the skills and activities that were taught

6. What two elements of your personality have assisted you most in your teaching?

_____

7. Given your responses and the list of teacher behaviors on page 32, write one sentence that emphasizes the behaviors that you would like to strengthen in your professional demeanor. _____

_____

Figure 2.2   Questions for practicing or experienced teachers.

From R.L Clements and A. Meltzer Rady, 2012, *Urban physical education: Instructional practices and cultural activities* (Champaign, IL: Human Kinetics).

display confidence and professionalism regardless of the hardships they encounter. They are also available and alert while continually circulating throughout the activity area to hear and see all that is happening in their class. They do not lean or sit during their instruction, since gymnasiums, unlike classrooms, do not have vantage points.

Teachers who display gravitas are more likely to handle off-task behavior before it gets out of hand or is imitated by a peer group. This may mean limiting the extent to which the teacher uses humor, adds personal anecdotes, or even grins and appears cheerful while conveying sport content to large groups of students in order to maintain constant respect from students or risk losing their class control. Moreover, maintaining a strong presence in the gymnasium greatly decreases the likelihood of physical outbursts and fights. Therefore displaying behaviors that reflect confidence such as keeping the head up, standing up straight, moving about, and having a voice that carries, as well as managing resources, taking action, and acting decisively, ranks high in the professional demeanor of many urban teachers.

Over time, a teacher's self-confidence in his ability to handle different situations increases, and the individual becomes more desensitized toward small things that often shake the composure of new teachers. This is one reason many school administrators and veteran teachers caution against new teachers' outwardly exhibiting too much empathy toward a student's personal strife, which can include previous criminal actions, incarceration of family members, and other family tragedies, to decrease the risk of becoming overwhelmed or even of teacher burnout. Acquiring gravitas helps teachers govern themselves and maintain a professional demeanor at all times.

No Matter the Circumstances . . .

Get up,
dress up, and
show up
for your students because they matter.

Model Your Expectations

* Whenever possible, physically participate with the students.
* Show genuine effort when conveying teaching cues.
* Respect limitations with a smile.
* Praise success and encourage additional practice.
* Check to see that the student understands, and welcome student feedback.

RESPONDING TO LIFE SKILLS QUESTIONS

Effective urban physical education teachers also place importance on conveying life skills. Life skills are informal skills that a troubled student can acquire by having a discussion with the teacher before or after the physical education class. These informal discussions usually help students think more clearly, feel more optimistic, act in an appropriate manner, and interact socially as participating members of society. For example, a teacher might identify specific health-related content to address acne to improve a student's physical appearance. Or a teacher could remind a student that coordination improves over time and that with additional practice the student's feelings of inadequacy should disappear. Or a teacher suggests that a student could have been better accepted by his classmates if he had used subtle interjections instead of yelling out his thoughts. In these three examples, the teacher responds to the student's issue to ease his anxiety about fitting in with peer groups.

However, life skill questions can focus on more serious social problems such as gang violence, teen alcoholism, teenage pregnancy, teenage suicide, student absenteeism and dropout rate, and HIV infection. Urban physical education teachers realize that the high incidence of social problems greatly influences their teaching environment, and their ability to comfortably convey life skills is critical to their teaching success. Life skills enable

Learning life skills can help students deal with and speak out about social problems such as violence in school.

the student *look* for assistance within the school (e.g., school counselor, school social worker, or nurse) and finally ask the student if she has had the opportunity to *learn* more about the topic from outside resources (e.g., a suggested Internet resource, a local office, an agency that can send free information).

After using these three basic life skill techniques, the teacher has the responsibility of contacting the immediate school administrator (e.g., department chairperson, assistant principal) and summarizing the issue and solutions that were suggested to the student. It is also helpful to have a bulletin board that displays the names of national agencies, services, and websites. Often students who have serious life skill problems take advantage of this information, especially in schools that do not offer health education classes. Urban physical education teachers frequently mention how resilient their students are given their personal predicaments. Resilience refers to the student's ability to adapt to hardship at school and in the home. Resilience depends on coping mechanisms and life skills such as problem solving, the ability to seek support, motivation, perseverance, and resourcefulness. Resilience is present when factors that support well-being are stronger than risk factors that cause harm.

individual students to adapt and deal effectively with the demands of adolescence when faced with challenging environmental and family conditions that can include coming from a low socioeconomic status and in some cases severe poverty and homelessness.

Teachers who take the time to convey life skills before or after the class session also realize that many students have stressful and sometimes verbally abusive home environments that influence their performance in school. Rather than assume the student can seek help at home or believe that this is some other teacher's responsibility, teachers can choose to implement three basic leadership skills referred to as listen, look, learn. First, the teacher *listens* to the student and is attentive even though many competing stimuli may demand attention. Teachers must realize that they may be the only adult of whom the student feels comfortable asking a question. A good way to proceed is to say, "Tell me briefly about your situation so that I can better understand you." The physical education teacher can then suggest that

Eight Beliefs and Practices of Effective Urban Physical Education Teachers

* Accept difficult challenges in the workplace
* Maintain high expectations for students' success
* Recognize the need to convey life skills
* Respect the student's resilience
* Use culturally responsible curricula
* Implement techniques to deescalate behavioral problems
* Reflect on and assess the objectives of lessons
* Feel genuine pride in even small accomplishments

Youth and Adolescents

In the United States, *youth* are people between 15 and 24 years, and *adolescents* are people between the ages of 10 and 19. Together they form the largest category of young people, those between 10 and 24 years of age. The end of adolescence and the beginning of adulthood vary. Within a country or culture, the ages at which an individual is considered mature enough to be entrusted by society with certain tasks can differ. Youth refers to a period during which the individual moves to greater independent responsibility. Definitions vary from one context to another depending on sociocultural, institutional, economic, and political factors.

RESPONDING TO BEHAVIORS WITH PRIDE

Most teachers and parents are familiar with the cliché, "Example is the best teacher." In the school setting, this can mean that whatever behavior a teacher displays toward his students will be mirrored. The saying also reinforces the need for teachers to resist the urge to engage in sarcastic comments, put-downs, or ridicule. It is critical that teachers remain professional at all times and not allow a student's behavior to trigger a personal reaction. A "trigger" is an action, event, or thing that evokes a personal response from the teacher resulting in verbal abuse or even corporal punishment. Triggers include student behaviors such as the following:

* Leaving or attempting to leave the gymnasium without a teacher's permission
* Being verbally rude or disrespectful
* Disrupting the educational process
* Using profanity or taking part in lewd acts
* Using racial, sexual, or ethnic slurs against a classmate
* Defying a teacher's directions and disobeying the teacher's authority

Happily, one of the best responses to an occasional inappropriate behavior is simply using a calm voice and asking the student by name to "be nice." This suggestion gives the student a "door to walk through," and many students will respond by saying something like "OK, OK" and stop the inappropriate behavior.

Unfortunately, however, many urban teachers face far more serious resistance with individuals who obstruct their teaching effectiveness. To avoid responding inappropriately, they must maintain a sense of professional pride as they react. Teachers can incorporate the acronym PRIDE into their repertoire: place, refrain, ignore, dismiss, and encourage.

1. **P**lace the behavior or action as the main focus of your response. Example: "Slamming the gymnasium door hard enough to break the hinges destroys school property and warrants a week's suspension, Samuel."

2. **R**efrain from revealing your frustration or anger. In fact, the greater the problem in the class setting, the greater the need to control your temper. When teachers react with anger to a student's behavior, they should turn away slightly or take a step back until they are composed and in clear control of their emotions. Some teachers refrain from revealing their frustration by saying, "I see you are very frustrated, Jolene, but . . . ," or "I can hear your anger, Jolene, but . . . ," or "I am not certain why you are saying that, Jolene, but . . ." followed by a description of the behavior. These responses help to defuse the teacher's behavior and the student's behavior in order to calm the situation.

3. **I**gnore the urge to yell at a student. There has never been a teacher who said, "I felt so much better after I blew up and shouted at a student." If a teacher must confront a student who is lashing out verbally, he should proceed slowly and quietly to where the student is and put one finger to his lips as a signal for the student to listen. He should ask the student to "please stop" shouting and then walk away. It is important for the teacher to remember that the student wants attention. If the student resists, the teacher should avoid making an issue of it. Rather, he reflects on the behavior (e.g., "Cursing out a classmate, pushing, and then grabbing the ball will not be tolerated, Hosea—find a seat") and then walks away. If any member of the class obstructs the teacher's task,

the situation must be treated calmly. The individual should be expected to either leave the class immediately (with advanced administrative approval) or preferably sit alone. At the first opportunity, the offense should be dealt with in a private conference.

4. **D**ismiss any thought of invading the space of a hostile student. Even touching a student's arm, shoulder, or back can raise the student's level of aggression and constitute a form of invasion. Student aggression is most often visible in the face, from disapproving frowns and pursed lips to sneers and full snarls. The eyes can be used to stare and hold a gaze for long time. Students may also squint, preventing the other person from seeing where they are looking. When a student is about to physically attack another student, he normally gives a visual signal such as clenching

of fists ready to strike and lowering and spreading of the body for stability. He is also likely to show anger signs such as redness of the face and chin tilting. All of these gestures may be sudden, signaling a level of aggression and testing the teacher's reactions. Avoid physical confrontations at all times.

5. **E**ncourage respectful interactions and avoid derogatory comments, which make a teacher appear less than a trained professional of high character. In general, teachers must strive to maintain a professional relationship even if a student has just shown a crude gesture, made a barbed comment, or yelled out a personal put-down. If a teacher is not certain about how to respond to an individual's difficult behavior, he should not do anything until he takes a moment to think. Common sense based on professional training will prevail.

When a student shows signs of aggression, react calmly and professionally and avoid invading the student's space.

Derogatory Messages to Avoid

* Ordering (e.g., "I said do it now, not tomorrow or when you feel like it")

* Interrogating ("What is your problem?"; "Is there something you want to tell the class?"; "Why is Sharonna upset? Did you have something to do with that?")

* Refusing to listen ("I don't want to hear any more excuses")

* Labeling ("fashion queen," "trouble maker," "class clown")

* Threatening ("You had better stop that or else"; "The next time, you're out of here"; "If you break that pedometer, you're buying it")

* Moralizing ("I won't be surprised if you never finish anything in your life")

Most schools offer in-service workshops focusing on class management techniques. All physical education teachers should be aware of their school's program and preferred routines. It is imperative that all teachers be on board with the same classroom management system. In the situation in which a school does not have a formal system, teachers should ask to review the school district's policy. All school districts in the United States are required to have a written plan, and urban schools usually have detailed plans. New York City, for example, has a 34-page document titled "Strategies for Preventing Corporal Punishment and Verbal Abuse." This document assists with understanding of corporal punishment and teacher violations. Chicago's school district offers its teachers a 61-page document titled "The DCPS Philosophy and Approach to Student Behavior and Discipline," devoted to a safe and effective learning environment, and includes eight additional pages on disciplinary response to student behavior. The Washington, DC, 55-page document is called "The Student Code of Conduct." Most school districts post their class management suggestions or guidelines on their website under the concept of student behavior, or teacher violations, or disciplinary actions.

COMMON TRIGGER SCENARIOS

The 10 physical education scenarios described in this section assist teachers in understanding student behaviors that could trigger a teacher's inappropriate reaction. Possible teacher responses are also provided.

Trigger: Profanity

Scenario

Jim had been an urban physical education teacher for two years. He was amazed at the frequency with which Peter and other students used profanity. He could not tell whether Peter swore intentionally or whether he was even aware that he was swearing. However, it was clear that Peter regarded swearing as a common way to communicate, while other students used it as a defensive tool. Others were clearly trying to maintain relationships by swearing in order to make their peer group aware of their presence. The shock value of hearing students call each other names or spout vulgar language had worn off. At first Jim was angered by the fact that his students did not care where or to whom they cursed. Experience had taught him to control his anger and to force himself to look beyond the words students used. A colleague had suggested that when he heard students using language he considered shocking, it would be best to find out whether it had the same meaning to students. Sometimes what is rough language to the teacher's ear may be the common way to express feelings where a particular student lives. This doesn't make abusive language acceptable, but it does give insight into a student's use of profanity and how to bring about change.

Suggested Responses

Recognize that there are two common situations behind swearing. The first involves students like Peter who continually swear but are not necessarily discipline problems, and therefore punishing them is not the key to changing their habit. The second involves students who swear as a defensive means to protect themselves against the teacher's punishment after they have violated a rule. In both cases it is important not to take the student's words personally or jump to any value judgments.

* "I know you are upset or you would not have said that, but let's not say that anymore." (The statement gives the student a second chance, and the teacher's dignity can be maintained.)

* "Your behavior is not acceptable in the gymnasium. How you speak outside the gym and school is your business, but not in here."

* "Swearing disturbs some students. Please find another way to express your feelings."

* "Please find a different word," or "Find another word to use."

* Remind the student that professional athletes must learn to control their tempers, and they often substitute greater physical effort to accomplish a task for boasting and profanity.

Trigger: Ongoing Excuses

Scenario

Tina had an excuse or alibi for everything. She never fulfilled her class responsibilities. She always seemed to feel that the fault rested on someone else. Even worse, Tina was very capable of presenting highly creative excuses.

Suggested Responses

Keep in mind that the student who always has an excuse has usually experienced ongoing failure with adult and peer interactions. Furthermore she has a tendency to feel that she has been treated unfairly by adults at school and at home. The student needs to belong to a group and develop close friends. Developing a sense of self-worth may change her behavior. Ask the student to discuss the habit, and learn what's really happening in her life. Explain that people must accept the consequences of their actions, that excuses do not relieve us of responsibility. Let the student know your expectations and make it clear that repeated alibis will not be accepted.

* "I cannot forget your actions just because you have an excuse."

* "The fact that you have an excuse does not change the fact that your actions have consequences."

* Prepare a simple written contract with the student and allow opportunity for the contract to succeed.

Trigger: Disrespect

Scenario

Evan expressed his disrespect with continual sighs, sneers, and looks of clear disdain. He also showed a total lack of common courtesy; and his gestures conveyed that he didn't think very highly of anyone, including himself, even though he might act superior. His ongoing frustration, anger, or hostility was a strong indication that his basic needs were not being met. Evan's teachers knew that fighting fire with fire could not change disrespect. A public confrontation in the gymnasium may put a student on the spot and compel him to act even worse to save face with his peer group and show that he doesn't get pushed around by anyone. Retaliating only lets him off the hook; it is much better to keep the responsibility on the student. An unprofessional reaction always reinforces negative behavior in a disrespectful student.

Suggested Responses

Disrespectful behavior is an indicator that a student has problems, is experiencing failure, has been hurt, or has been indulged too often by adults. It is quite possible that the student has been mistreated and therefore is acting in the same way toward others. Students at the secondary level often display disrespect by making brief offensive remarks, engaging in boastful behavior, being noisy, and ignoring the teacher's need to begin instruction. Disrespectful behavior can also include sarcasm toward the teacher.

* Ask, "What's wrong? Did I do something to offend you?" This question avoids fueling the situation and instead sets the stage to resolve it. Other students may not support disrespect directed at the teacher when the teacher responds respectfully.

* In cases in which a remark was completely unwarranted, say, "I don't think I deserve that. Now tell me what's really on your mind." This is confronting in a professional and caring way. This response will produce more instant student apologies and can resolve more ugly incidents than a negative or retaliatory reaction on the part of the teacher.

The Urban Teacher's Personal Mantra

Many teachers who work in high-stress situations find it useful to have a mantra to chant in their mind when student behavioral problems seem especially stressful. Examples of mantras of practicing teachers include "Never give up—never give in"; "Winners never quit"; "One day at a time"; "Great teachers do more"; and "Teach, don't talk." The point is to select or create a mantra that has a personal meaning. Mentors often pass on advice that becomes a part of a new teacher's mantra.

Trigger: Insistence on Having the Last Word

Scenario

Jackson persisted in saying one more thing or laughing, sneering, or sighing even when he knew this behavior would lead to trouble. He sought attention at any price and was often inconsiderate, even making excuses for his actions. Jackson's need for power was the main cause of his disruptive behavior. His feelings of athletic or academic ineptness prompted his desire to have the last word. Jackson needed to learn how to channel his assertiveness in a positive direction and feel empowered. The physical education teacher knew that it was senseless to talk to him in the presence of his peers other than to say, "We will chat later, Jackson," since Jackson really didn't want to reason and craved attention at all costs. He had already prejudged who liked him and who didn't as well as who was strong and who was weak. He behaved better with those he regarded as strong.

Suggested Responses

Students who display this behavior often monopolize the teacher's attention and may have an exaggerated opinion of their importance.

* Remain calm and poised even if totally shaken by the student's action; give a quick

smile in the student's direction and then turn immediately to another student.

* When talking to the student in private, use the major issue technique. Tell the student that you recognize his need for attention but that there are acceptable ways to obtain approval. Explain that the student's responsibility is to function on a more mature level. Then talk about your responsibility to this student and to the class. Say, "Even though I don't want to embarrass you publicly, I cannot tolerate behavior that steals time from your classmates."

* Reinforce the difference between assertion and aggression. Through assertion a student voices his opinion and speaks out without hurting others. Aggressive acts infringe upon the rights of others.

Trigger: Constant Interruptions

Scenario

Lucia had a comment for every teacher direction. She had an opinion on everything, mumbled comments under her breath, and frequently laughed at inappropriate times. Clearly she was trying very hard to gain status with her peers by attempting to establish relationships and choosing to make herself known by interrupting in class. She was struggling to assert herself through constant interruptions. Her message was loud and clear: "Recognize me, I'm here."

Suggested Responses

Students who continually interrupt the class process are exhibiting behavior that interferes with others' right to learn. This behavior can include interruptive questioning of the teacher during the teacher's (or another student's) presentation of a physical skill. Another form of interruptive behavior is persistent talking when a meaningful classroom dialogue is taking place.

* In a private conference with the student, identify her obvious strengths and convey that others think well of her. Tell her that her comments are disrupting the flow of the class.

* In extreme cases, explain that the student's interruptions are breaking up both the teaching and learning sequences, and you will not allow them to continue.

Take aside a student who constantly interrupts the class and explain your position in private. Disciplining her in front of her peers only gives her the attention she seeks.

Trigger: Rabble-Rousing

Scenario

Gustavo's physical education teacher had never thought of him as a leader of a cause, but Gustavo certainly had the ability to encourage his classmates to raise petty grievances against the teacher. He also felt very comfortable pitting some students against others while acting as an innocent bystander. He never failed to stir up trouble as a way of seeking attention. Clearly, Gustavo desired to belong to a group, but his inability to be a successful leader caused him to seek attention by being a rabble-rouser.

Suggested Responses

Students who are rabble-rousers find false identity by taking advantage of any opportunity to arouse others to action. Their goal is to provoke, excite, and stimulate discussion that can quickly take attention away from the lesson. The behavior can be as subtle as a provocative smile, or the student can blatantly urge others not to participate or follow the teacher's directions.

* When confronting the student, identify the issue quickly and do not allow him to generalize and wander off topic. Ask him to pinpoint his complaint, and then reinforce that the problem stems from within himself and that he should work for a solution privately.

* Explain that you will also involve others including the school's administrators and parents. Tell the student that he has the right to complain and help resolve the issue but not to simply stir up and create a problem.

Trigger: Aggression

Scenario

Terry had developed a reputation as an overly aggressive student. He was highly emotional and quick-tempered, and he had tried to intimidate his peers as a way of getting attention. When his classroom teachers confronted him about his behavior, he usually claimed that he never got a fair deal. His grades dropped the more he became anti-PE, anti-school, and anti-teacher. He demonstrated these feelings through verbal abuse and open defiance. He was very revengeful and was disliked by his peers.

Suggested Responses

Students with very low self-esteem often try to cover it up with aggressive behavior. Aggressive behavior differs from assertive behavior in that aggression includes some intent to harm another person. People can learn behaviors like aggression by watching and imitating the behavior of others. Many educators suggest that the violence on television, in movies, and in mature-rated computer games increases the likelihood of short-term aggression. High-risk students may have also witnessed aggressive acts in their home setting and may have come to believe that these acts are acceptable.

* The aggressive student often dismisses the teacher's or student's suggestions and does not maintain loyalties to friends. Since students think that aggression is the way to get what they want, teachers should slow them down by using calming words. An aggressive reaction is different from a hostile response.

* Whenever possible, provide opportunities for success and talk to the aggressor. Most teachers avoid students who are behaving aggressively. Show sincere concern, and never return bad manners or behavior since this demonstrates a lack of control.

* Show strong displeasure with the behavior, and explain the difference between assertion and aggression (e.g., "With aggression, people walk over people to get what they want, whereas it is often OK to assert yourself because that doesn't hurt anyone else").

Trigger: Anger

Scenario

Bela appeared to be mad at herself and others most of the time. The anger that she displayed varied in intensity, but it was constant. She did not hesitate to lash out verbally and physically at her classmates and teachers in physical education classes. When confronted, she became defensive regarding the reason for her anger; she believed she was justified, which caused her to become even more angry toward the person who did see her viewpoint. Throughout her childhood she had thrown tantrums and blamed others for causing her anger. She had never learned to act out her frustrations in a positive manner.

Suggested Responses

Anger is an emotion that is most often displayed through feelings of displeasure and hostility. At the worse end of the spectrum, students can become enraged and use physical force to act on these emotions. Anger and irritability can be signs of an underlying mental health condition, such as depression or bipolar disorder. As a first step, teachers must address the need for students to recognize and manage their anger.

* Attempts should be made to give Bela responsibility, as long as she can maintain self-control. She could be placed in a small leadership role or a role of responsibility within a small group and acknowledged when she is successful.

* Threatening this student has an opposite effect, since she will get angrier and may respond by saying something like "I don't care what you do to me." Sarcasm directed toward Bela will also fuel this type of response.

* Tell Bela, "I feel sorry that you always seem to be angry. What can I do to help?" This response often helps since few adults show empathy for this person and Bela does not want people to pity her because this makes her feel inferior to other students. This student likes to believe that she has self-control, so appeal to this need after saying that you feel sorry.

* The best time to talk to Bela is when she is not upset. Point out to her that she is easygoing and is a good student when she isn't angry. Focus on the idea of learning to control her anger, and avoid saying that it is bad or wrong to be angry all the time or she will block future talks.

* Look her in the eye, listen, and wait until she has finished talking. If possible, don't interrupt, and give Bela a chance to let the anger dissolve.

* Do not expect immediate change in the gymnasium, since anger is a strong emotion that can be based on psychological problems requiring professional school counseling.

Trigger: Bullying

Scenario

Jose did not hesitate to verbally and physically push his classmates around in physical education, and he was happy to make good on his threats outside of the school setting. He had a bad temper and a bad mouth, and his lack of self-concept seemed best served when he was putting down peers who were smaller, weaker, or physically impaired. He found it satisfying to degrade others and humiliate weaker classmates. He often bragged about how his goal was to become a gang member. Jose was an attention seeker and liked being noticed by his peers and school officials.

Suggested Responses

Since bullies demonstrate their need for power by physically or verbally abusing others, it is important to remember that Jose can establish a relationship only by being the strongest, and he adopts bullying behavior for protection from others. Exerting or threatening to exert his physical strength makes this student feel independent and in charge of his life.

* If Jose threatens to "get someone" after class, hold him after class. Confront him and say, "You made a threat in my class and if you carry it out, please be prepared to face the full consequences."
* Keep in mind that most bullies are weak and may be using threats and actions to cover up insecurity.
* Whenever possible, establish a one-to-one relationship with Jose, people who bully often lack a strong and successful adult model.
* When communicating with Jose, be calm and speak softly, since a bully cannot respond or fight back as easily when the communication is gentle.
* Openly address the need for the student to rechannel his energies constructively, and provide activities that can bring out his leadership qualities in a positive way.

* Avoid putting the student in a position in which he must "prove" himself, or the bullying behavior is to likely continue.
* Take advantage of the fact that athletics are a good outlet for this behavior. Get the student involved.

Trigger: Constant Talking

Scenario

Sheronda was a compulsive talker and made irrelevant comments at inappropriate times. Her strong social need for personal interaction was based on her need to experience success through talking and to have others think that she was "somebody." This craving for attention through nonstop talking was really more a social problem than a discipline problem.

Suggested Responses

Students who talk incessantly throughout a class may not actually contribute to the needs or interests of the group. People sometimes warn friends about being a "motor mouth," which is a fun way of saying the person dominates conversations. However, constant talking can be a sign of a real social limitation that should be addressed by caring physical education teachers.

* Approach Sheronda's compulsive talking behavior as a social problem, not a discipline problem. Do not assume that Sheronda knows her ongoing behavior is inappropriate.
* Be consistent with the amount of attention you give this student regarding her problem and suggest private counseling.
* The talker has a strong activity need. Give her small tasks and responsibilities in the gymnasium to fulfill this need.
* When this student is talking, it is better to walk toward her, make eye contact several times, or call on her rather than stopping the class and bringing attention to her.
* If the behavior persists, find an opportunity for a private conversation and say, "I think you need to limit the amount of talking that you do in class to only those times that require partner or whole-group work." Reinforce that the student has strengths in a particular sport or wellness activity, but her ongoing talking makes it difficult for some students to concentrate and she must stop.

Even More Behaviors

Over time, teachers are confronted with numerous student behaviors that extend beyond those discussed here. For more detailed information, readers can refer to several educational leadership websites for principals and deans of students. One example is www.masterteacher.com.

GANGS IN URBAN SCHOOLS

From an educational standpoint, the term *gang* refers to a group of students who spend their social time together, act in concert for social cohesion and mutual protection from violent neighborhoods, or sometimes engage in a course or pattern of criminal activity for profit. Members share a common name or identity and have identifying clothing, symbols, and signs. The activity of gangs most often takes place in predetermined or general meeting areas in urban settings. Schools throughout the United States must take many precautions to ensure that the actions of gangs are not part of the school environment. The following information can assist teachers who are not familiar with characteristics associated with gang behavior.

Identifying Gang Involvement

Dressing differently can be an indication of gang involvement if a student wears only one type or brand of clothing; a particular jacket; or accessories such as bandanas, rosaries, or chains. Some gangs have one pant leg shorter than the other. One or more specific shave lines into one or both eyebrows or in the hair, or a particular tattoo, may distinguish a gang member. Enforce school dress codes that prohibit displaying gang colors or paraphernalia, and maintain physical education dress codes.

In some large cities, community gang intervention counselors monitor students before and after school to help prevent fights and other social disturbances.

Gang involvement can also mean talking differently, employing slang or made-up words. *Bigarette* is a word for cigarette in gangs that substitute the letter *b* for *c*. Teachers sometimes overhear students mentioning fighting, knives, switchblades, guns, crime events, or gang names. Report this behavior to the school officials.

Members of gangs are quickly taught new attitudes. Individuals may display a new sense of bravado or machismo or be confrontational, distanced, hostile, or arrogant in physical education class.

Ripped and torn clothing and visible bruises are typical characteristics of gang life. It is not uncommon for gang members to settle arguments aggressively. More violence occurs when small weapons are added to prove one's viewpoint. Sadly, deaths occur within gangs at an alarming rate.

Teachers should be aware that teens join gangs because they give an individual a sense of belonging, excitement, and heightened reputation. This belonging, however, usually involves criminal acts, underage drinking, vandalism, drug abuse, shoplifting, drug sales, assaults, rape, and other organized crimes and violence. The process of "jumping out," in which all gang members beat someone up, is an indication of the violence. Physical education teachers can post information from Striving To Reduce Youth Violence Everywhere (STRYVE), available at www.safeyouth.gov.

Recognizing Gang Tattoos

The word tattoo is taken from the Tahitian word *tatu*. Tattoos are used to identify people in many cultures and in street gangs. Gang tattoos often have one or more distinguishing symbols of gang affiliation, or gang members may wear multiple tattoos to signify that they have spent time in prison. These include spider webs, which indicate prison time, or phrases such as *thug life*. All teachers working in middle and high schools should recognize gang tattoos in contrast to personalized tattoos worn by members of the general public.

Area Code Tattoos

The area code for the city or area where the gang is situated is often used as a gang identifier. Some examples of well-known area codes are 213 (Los Angeles), 415 (San Francisco), 718 (Bronx), 212 (Manhattan), 817 (Fort Worth), and 614 (Columbus).

Aryan Brotherhood Gang Tattoos

The Aryan Brotherhood, which is also known as AB or The Brand, is basically a white prison gang with about 15,000 members in and out of prison. Members of these gangs use symbols in their tattoos such as swastikas, SS lightning bolts, the number 666, and Celtic imagery.

Black Gang Tattoos

The Black Guerilla Family is a prison gang founded in 1966 by Black Panther George Jackson while he was in prison. The most common tattoo is BGF; another is the numerals 276, where the number 2 represents B, 7 represents G, and 6 represents F.

Hispanic Gang Tattoos

One of the popular images among Hispanic gang members is a five-point crown on the upper arm. Another common Hispanic tattoo is a small five-point star, usually on the hand between the thumb and the first finger.

Mexican and Latin Gang Tattoos

Mexican gang tattoos and other Latin gang tattoos frequently reflect the religious background or blood ties of a gang. The common praying hands tattoo represents praying for forgiveness for one's actions. Another common tattoo is Lady of Guadalupe, a popular saint of many Hispanics.

Japanese Gang Tattoos

These tattoos most often take the form of simple black rings around the arm, one ring for each crime a gang member has committed. Japanese tattoos are very distinctive because the faces of Japanese warriors are commonly represented.

Vietnamese Gang Tattoos

Since tattoos are fairly new to the Vietnamese, many gang members identify themselves by other body alteration, such as cigarette burns on their hands or ankles. One exception is the initials NCA, which stand for Ninja Clan Assassin.

Teardrop Tattoo and Dot Tattoos

The teardrop tattoo worn under one eye may have originated with Hispanic gangs in California in the 1940s. Initially, it was believed that the wearer of the teardrop tattoo had spent time in prison. Today, gang members use it to signify toughness.

Dot tattoos are most commonly located on the finger webs, the elbows, and the wrists. Three dots

Sample Names of Urban Gangs in the United States

Bloods

Crips

Gangster Disciples

Latin Kings

Flying Dragons

Netas

Dominicans Don't Play

Trinitarios

Ninos Malos

Squadron

Chicano Nation

in a triangular shape often reflect the only three places gang members go: the hospital, the prison, and the grave. A tattoo of three dots in a triangle, usually located between the thumb and forefinger, may represent the 3 *I*s of the gang culture: injury, incarceration, and internment.

PROTOCOLS FOR TEACHING LARGE CLASSES

One of the oldest definitions of the term *protocol* comes from the Greek word *kolla,* meaning glue, used to bind sheets of papyrus together. The prefix, *proto* extended the concept to holding things more tightly together and *maintaining a procedure.* The word *protocol* is more commonly used than the earlier term "school rules," and it is frequently used in research on leadership skills and class management techniques for older students. Protocols represent specific behaviors and actions that a teacher repeatedly implements to ensure presentation of an effective lesson. They increase the likelihood that the teacher will stay organized throughout the lesson and that the students will adhere to a positive code of conduct.

The protocols described in this section were identified by experienced urban teachers who work with large class sizes. They are discussed according to three categories: preliminary protocols, performance protocols, and assessment protocols. The key is to maintain each protocol in every lesson. This is possible because each facet of the lesson includes only five recommended protocols, and most teachers are able to commit them to memory. Students also become alert to many of the protocols and recognize that they reflect the teacher's ongoing class procedure and expectations. In any case, the "less is best" idea has seemed to serve as the "glue" used by many successful urban teachers when they are confronted with the numerous variables and distractions of large classes.

Preliminary Protocols

Good planning requires a preparatory step or an initial series of actions to prevent problems from ever occurring in a classroom. The following preliminary protocols are especially effective when working with large groups to decrease the likelihood of chaos occurring at the beginning of the class.

1. *Acquire and organize available equipment to prevent student restlessness.* It is helpful if the teacher mentally runs through the lesson sequence beforehand to determine if adequate equipment is available and if there is a need for an air pump, cones, a CD player, or some other piece of equipment that could be overlooked. The equipment should be placed near the teacher in an equipment bag, a crate, or some other type of container. This decreases students' temptation to take the equipment and play with it before the lesson begins.

2. *Greet the students at the door.* The teacher's presence will remind the students that behavior in class differs from that in an athletic setting.

3. *Use a specific signal to begin the class to indicate that all students must be quiet and attentive.* This signal should not change, and it can be as simple a hand raised over the head or a particular whistle.

4. *Reinforce the lesson's primary objective.* Most teachers accomplish this by saying, "The purpose of today's activity is . . ."; they typically include at least one new advanced sport skill or health-related concept so that students become accustomed to hearing new terminology. Repeat words several times for English language learners if necessary.

To keep lessons organized and encourage restless students to stay on point, plan to have all necessary equipment available at the start of class.

5. *Convey the origin of the activity or some historical sport fact.* This sparks interest and increases the students' understanding of the cultures, identities, and histories of the diverse groups that participate in sport and compose our society.

Performance Protocols

Performance protocols focus on elements of the lesson that are explicitly instructional. These protocols tend to be used at the beginning of the lesson when the skills are introduced. Exceptional teachers never become "spectators" as the lesson proceeds but instead continue to implement performance protocols until its very end. The following are common performance protocols that work especially well in urban settings.

1. *Make use of a teacher, student demonstration, or photograph to model the correct way to perform an advanced physical activity or motor skill.*

2. *Use nondiscriminatory partner and group selection techniques and international skill formations that do not create identifiably racial, ethnic, or gender groups to practice a new skill.* (For details, see chapter 1.)

3. *Provide a trial demonstration of the game or activity using a small group of students to alleviate any confusion concerning the rules or skills, or demonstrate with a whole-group activity.* It may also be necessary to use this trial as a way of preventing the most skilled students from dominating the activity. The trial game gives the teacher the opportunity to identify, for instance, a specific number of passes that students must make before shooting a goal. It could also allow the teacher to identify the playing positions that must make contact with the ball before a goal is scored to ensure full participation, since the teacher must avoid rules that refer to either sex (e.g., a girl must touch the ball at least once in order for the goal to count).

4. *Insist on cooperative gestures (a handshake, a closed handshake, or a high five) before a competitive activity; discourage slang, ethnic name calling, and any crude comments while also applauding and praising group success.*

5. *Continually circulate throughout the playing area, praise individuals, serve as a model when needed, give constant feedback, and observe the students' level of success.*

Assessment Protocols

Effective teachers are always searching for ways to make a lesson more meaningful to their students. Keeping students on task is a great challenge for urban physical education teachers. No amount of planning can be effective unless the teacher assesses which lesson items have worked well and which items need to be revised.

1. *Decide in the first few class sessions which (if any) protocols need to be revised or expanded.* Many urban teachers and numerous coaches live by the saying, "Never change a winning game, only a losing one."

2. *Ask a colleague to assess your idiosyncrasies and mannerisms (e.g., the use of "OK," "guys," "gonna," or "all right?"), and whether any small acts of group misbehavior were overlooked.* Teachers must be clear, concise, and on task but not overlook behavior problems. The lack of response to serious infractions sends the message that the teacher is condoning poor behavior and takes away from the teacher's instruction.

3. *Ask any wavering students, "What color stick would you like?" or "What position would you like to play?" Avoid asking a student if he wants to play.* Maintaining 80 percent student participation is very difficult in class sizes of over 70 students. However, the best urban teachers strive every day to get one more student involved.

4. *Use teacher refection and several forms of authentic assessment techniques to appraise*

the lesson's success and to conclude whether the students were encouraged to feel responsibility for the lesson's success. It is especially important that individual students feel they play a role in the lesson's success. See chapter 5 of this book for sample rubrics.

5. *Determine whether the students are following a dismissal protocol that prevents a dismissal riot.* Consider using statements such as this: "All students with the letters *c*, *d*, and *l* in their first names may leave now."

SUMMARY

All middle and high school teachers in the United States can expect their students to have certain concerns and show certain behaviors that are a part of adolescence. Often students (a) have social concerns that dominate their thoughts and activities; (b) are self-conscious, moody, restless, and easily bored; (c) display loyalty to their friends and sometimes cruelty to classmates outside their circle of friends; and (d) are easily offended and very sensitive to criticism regarding their shortcomings.

However, urban physical education teachers confront numerous behaviors that are not common to all gymnasiums in rural areas. In many urban schools, the teacher has no choice but to display a firm teacher demeanor since the class size can be as large as 100. In this situation, the percentage of high-risk students is likely to be higher, so the need to respond to life skill questions is greater. The severity of behavioral problems, including those of students affiliated with gangs, is also likely to trigger the teacher's strong opposition and take the teacher's attention away from the lesson's objectives. Therefore, carefully followed protocols become an important element of the urban physical education teacher's style of leadership. Many educators believe "Those who can do. Those willing to do more teach urban physical education."

PART TWO

PHYSICAL EDUCATION ACTIVITIES FOR URBAN SETTINGS

CULTURALLY DIVERSE ACTIVITIES AND CHALLENGES

Numerous students in the United States today take diversity for granted because many have a diverse group of friends, and others come from cross-cultural families. However, even in ideal educational settings, one of the biggest challenges teachers face is learning how to effectively and sensitively teach students from different cultures. This can be especially true in urban physical education settings having large class sizes, mixed ability groups, numerous languages, and differing physical experiences.

Whenever possible, the physical education teacher should get a sense of how students feel about the cultural climate in the gymnasium. Individuals can be asked to speak after class to share ideas, express concerns, identify negative aspects of activities, suggest rule modifications, identify activities that cause them to feel uncomfortable, or identify whether they think some groups of students receive preferential treatment. All students should be respected equally, and all teachers must strive to avoid making assumptions about students' attentiveness based on their physical appearance, eye contact, command of English, and ethnic background.

This consideration is very important when teachers are striving to create a learning environment where differences are recognized, understood, and valued so that all middle and high school students can perform physical activity skills to their fullest potential. One way to increase the likelihood of achieving this goal is to expand the middle and high school curriculum to include a variety of culturally diverse activities. Typically these activities have various origins, involve unique rules, and make use of many of the skills reflected in a variety of team and individual sports played in the United States and throughout the world. These goals directly coincide with two of the practices identified in *Appropriate Instructional Practice Guidelines for High School Physical Education*, published by the National Association for Sport and Physical Education (2009a):

1.4 Diversity

1.4.1 Appropriate Practice

The physical educator creates an environment that is inclusive and supportive of all students, regardless of race, ethnic origin, gender, sexual orientation, religion or physical ability.

These differences are acknowledged, appreciated, and respected.

1.4.2 Teachers intentionally select activities (e.g., dance and games from throughout the world) that represent a culturally diverse environment.

In addition to these practices, the authors of this book gave strong attention to *Moving Into the Future: National Standards for Physical Education* (National Association for Sport and Physical Education 2004) to select only activities and information that reflect those standards. While all of the standards were used as a guideline in the decision to select each activity, clearly the greatest attention focused on standards 1, 5, and 6:

A physically educated person:

1. *Demonstrates competency in motor skills and movement patterns needed to perform a variety of physical activities.*

2. Demonstrates understanding of movement concepts, principles, strategies, and tactics as they apply to the learning and performance of physical activities.

3. Participates regularly in physical activity.

4. Achieves and maintains a health-enhancing level of physical fitness.

5. *Exhibits responsible personal and social behavior that respects self and others in physical activity settings.*

6. *Values physical activity for health, enjoyment, challenge, self-expression, and/ or social interaction.*

Reprinted from National Association for Sport and Physical Education, 2004, *Moving into the future: National standards for physical education,* 2nd ed. (Reston, VA: NASPE).

With this understanding, curriculum developers should have an additional rationale for implementing and deciding on the value of the following culturally diverse physical activities that contain similar advanced skills to those found in basketball, bowling, handball, golf, soccer, softball, baseball, and volleyball, as well as several culturally diverse physical challenges in their school setting.

African Bolo Ball
AFRICA

→ Origin and Purpose

Soccer (footbol) is undoubtedly the most-loved sport within the countries of Africa. Netball, which is similar to basketball but without the basketball backboard, also has league and tournament play. Less is known about African bolo ball, in which players use a basketball and basketball skills to scoop the ball into the goal. In African bolo ball the students advance a basketball down a field, using only one hand to pass and dribble to teammates, and shoot at a goal taped on a wall. When a wall or large goal is not available, players can shoot at a basketball hoop instead. This modification is very appealing to students.

→ **Activity Area**

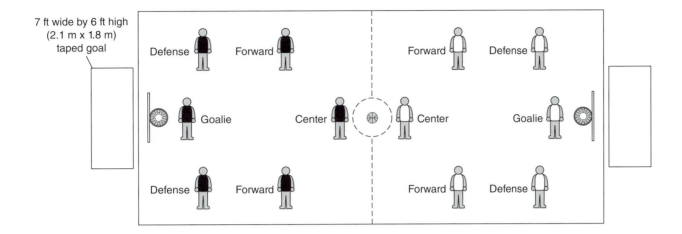

7 ft wide by 6 ft high (2.1 m x 1.8 m) taped goal

→ **Equipment**

One basketball, two taped goals or a basketball court

→ **Teaching Process**

1. A rectangle 7 feet (2.1 m) wide and 6 feet (1.8 m) high is taped on each wall at opposite ends of the playing area. These rectangles are the goals.

2. The students are organized in groups of six. Each group is composed of one center, two forwards, two defense players, and one goalkeeper.

3. Play begins when the teacher bounces a basketball on the floor in the center of the midcircle. The ball should not bounce higher than each center player's chest level, and both centers may try to snatch the ball as soon as it reaches their waist level.

4. Players advance the ball by using an overhand tap, by smashing it downward, by performing a sloping throw off the floor, or by bouncing the ball off an upper body part or any of the gymnasium's four walls. Players may also dribble the ball, as in basketball, for three bounces before stopping and passing the ball.

5. If the ball is kicked, a foul is awarded and the opposing team receives possession.

6. The goalie is the only player who can use both hands to block a ball. The goalie tries to prevent the opposing forward from scoring one point. He may also try to score a goal by throwing the ball to a forward, who attempts to score. Only one hand is permitted in the throwing action.

7. The object is to be the first group to score 10 points. The ball is bounced in the center of the midcircle by the teacher after each score.

8. In large classes, use a regulation basketball court with two baskets. Students (teams of six) try to dribble, pass, shoot, and score a basket using only one hand. In this version, the goalie waits back and tries to get a major opportunity at rebounding missed shots. Use a team substitution each time a basket is scored. This is a vigorous passing game.

→ Closure

Ask the students how difficult it was to use only one hand to advance and shoot the ball.

Egyptian Group Bowling
EGYPT

→ Origin and Purpose

Games related to bowling can be traced back to 5200 B.C. in Egypt, where archaeologists have found stone balls and ninepins in a child's tomb. The Dutch brought bowling to America in the 1660s. America's first indoor bowling alley opened in 1840 in Manhattan, New York. Paeng Nepomuceno, born in the Philippines in 1957, is acknowledged worldwide as the greatest international bowler in the history of the sport. Egyptian group bowling is played with a large number of students who score points collectively.

→ Activity Area

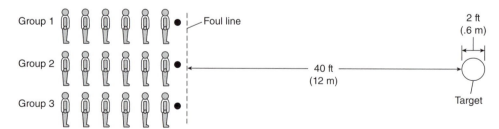

→ Equipment

Six to eight softballs (or tennis balls or street balls)

➜ Teaching Process

1. Construct a playing area 40 feet (12 m) or more long. Draw a foul line at one end of the field, and draw a circle 2 feet (.6 m) wide (the target) at the other end. Groups of six to eight students form lines, and all lines face the target.

2. The first student in each group bowls a softball or tennis ball at the target. The object is to roll the ball so it stops within the target.

3. After each student has bowled the ball, the score is tallied according to its end location. For example, the student whose ball stops nearest the center of the target earns 6 points for her group, the next closest student scores 5 points, and so on.

4. Students agree to play for 50, 70, or 100 points.

5. Mark the tennis balls with numbers, letters, or words for easier team identification.

6. It is helpful if each group has one person who keeps score.

7. A player may try to get her ball into the target as well as knock another person's ball out of the target. This is a strategic aspect of the game.

➜ Closure

Ask the students if they were able to demonstrate a positive attitude even when their score was lower or higher than that of others.

Fives

IRELAND

➜ Origin and Purpose

Fives is a British sport believed to have the same origin as many racket sports. The name fives may be derived from the slang expression "a bunch of fives," representing a fist. The game is also known as hand tennis. Fives involves partners hitting a tennis ball back and forth over a neutral area using their hands. Students may use an underhand serve, a forehand, a volley, or a smash to alternate hits.

➜ Activity Area

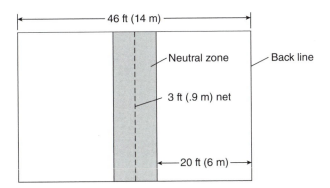

➜ Equipment

Net 3 feet (.9 m) high, measuring tape, masking tape, tennis balls, chalk

→ Teaching Process

1. Partners use a measuring tape and chalk to create the court. Two wooden chairs with a strip of masking tape attached to the top back of each chair can substitute for a 3-foot net. Each court should include chalk or tape for a back line.
2. Play begins when the student uses an underhand serve from behind the back line.
3. Scoring is possible only if the student is serving.
4. Both students continue to volley the ball until one or the other is unable to return it into the receiving area.
5. Balls cannot be served or played in the neutral zone.
6. Individuals agree to play to 10, 15, or 20 points.
7. Fives may be played as a singles game or a doubles game. A group of several students may practice hitting over the net as a warm-up activity.

→ Closure

Ask the students which technique (serve, rally, volley, or smash) they think needs the greatest amount of practice to improve performance and allow them to continue to play.

El Circulo Handball
SPAIN

→ Origin and Purpose

In 1050, French monks played *jeu de paume,* which meant hitting a ball with the palm of the hand. In 1861, before becoming president, Abraham Lincoln played handball in a vacant street lot near his law office. El circulo handball uses the skills of serving, volleying, smashing, and the forehand stroke to hit a tennis ball into a circular area. Partners volley the tennis ball until one student makes it impossible for the other to return the ball.

→ Activity Area

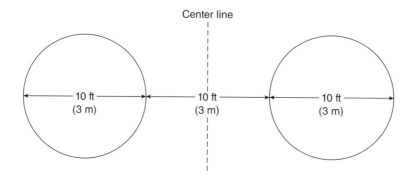

➜ Equipment

Measuring tape, string, chalk, handballs or tennis balls

➜ Teaching Process

1. Partners use a measuring tape, string, and chalk to create a two-circle court with a center line located between the two circles.

2. Play begins with two students standing on opposite sides of the center line and positioned outside the circle on their side of the court—that is, student 1 stands behind circle 1, and student 2 stands behind circle 2.

3. The serving student must use an underhand serve to put the tennis ball in play.

4. When student 1 serves the ball, the ball must first bounce inside circle 2. If student 1 serves the ball and it lands inside circle 2, then student 2 must hit the ball back so it first bounces inside circle 1. The players continue to hit the ball into the opposing player's circle. When a player fails to hit the ball so it bounces first in the other's circle the play ends and it's the other player's turn to serve.

5. A student earns a point only during the play following his own serve.

6. Neither student may cross the center line to return the ball.

7. The player's service ends after 5 serves.

8. The students must agree whether the game is to be won by the first player to reach 10, 15, or 20 points.

9. **Extension:** In partner el circulo handball, two teams play, each with two partners. Only one player on each team can be outside the circle at a time. The players on each team rotate in and out of the circle; the student hitting the ball must move inside the circle, and the other student moves outside the circle to make the next hit.

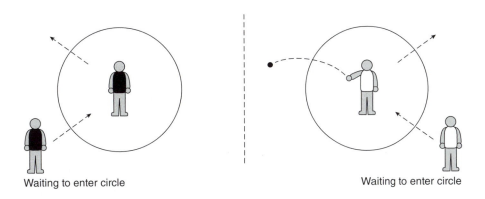

Waiting to enter circle   Waiting to enter circle

➜ Closure

Ask the students whether they were able to maintain their effort throughout the game or whether they allowed the other player or team to defeat them easily.

Scottish Clock Golf
SCOTLAND

→ Origin and Purpose

It is generally recognized that golf had its beginnings in Scotland, where shepherds hit round stones with long knotted sticks. The Scottish word *goulf* means to strike, and *divot* refers to a piece of turf. Mary, Queen of Scots, was said to be the first woman to play the game. In clock golf, students use a putting stroke similar to that in present-day golf and strive to complete a 12-hole course with the least number of putts while demonstrating patience during the wait for their next turn. With this game, minimal equipment is required to bring golf—a sport usually associated with lavish greens and ample space—to a city school.

> ## Tournament Action
>
> Top world golf tournaments include the British Open, U.S. Open, U.S. PGA Championship, U.S. Masters, Ryder Cup (males), and Curtis Cup (females).

→ Activity Area

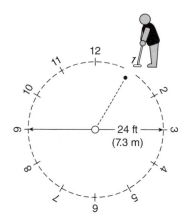

→ Equipment

Four to six putter irons, four to six golf balls, 12 markers, one tin container (e.g., an empty coffee can), pencil and paper for keeping score

Teaching Process

1. To design the clock golf course, place 12 markers at equal distances from each other in a path forming the circumference of a complete circle that has a radius of 24 feet (7.3 m). Number each marker as for a clock, 1 through 12. Place one tin container in the middle of the circle (24 feet from each marker).

2. Students should be given instructions regarding the proper grip for the golf club. The interlocking grip is a basic grip style in which the little finger (pinkie) of one hand (the right hand for a right-handed player) is hooked around or overlaps the index finger of the other hand. This is similar to shaking hands with the club. The palms face each other. The grip should be firm but not tight, and very little or no body movement should occur with putting.

3. Students practice several times and observe each other's putting grip for accuracy. The ball must be struck with the head of the putter, never pushed.

4. Students start from any numbered marker on the circumference of the circle and attempt to score a hole in one (i.e., get the ball into the tin cup). As many as six students at a time can be at each marker. These six students can also work with partners so that a total of 12 students can play at each clock diagram. As one student putts, the partner can keep score. A student must "hole out" (i.e., get the ball into the cup) from each marker before moving on to the next marker.

5. Scores are recorded on a sheet of paper identifying each hole and the number of shots it took for players to hole out.

6. If more than one student is playing from the same marker, they should alternate turns.

7. Field hockey sticks and balls may be substituted if golf equipment is not available. Multiple clocks can be created for greater participation.

8. The object is to be the player with the lowest score after the completion of all 12 holes.

Closure

Ask the students if they demonstrated patience while completing their strokes and waiting their turn.

Chinese Soccer
CHINA

Origin and Purpose

Soldiers in ancient China played *tsu-ch-iu* as part of their training, using the head of an enemy soldier as a ball. By the third century B.C. the Chinese used a stuffed ball made of leather, and then in later times used an inflated ball so that it carried farther. The early English players often used the gates of churches as goals. Early soccer balls consisted of an inflated pig's bladder encased within tanned leather. They were not waterproof, and the players used rawhide laces to stitch the last panel. The world-famous soccer player Pelé was born in Brazil. During his career in Brazil he scored more than 1,000 goals, and he later played with the New York Cosmos.

→ Teaching Process

1. Select three or four students to serve as "builders" who have the task of creating a fence (palificata) of players. These four students stand in the middle of the playing area. (For a smaller class, use two students as the builders.) Their task is to continually kick soccer balls out of play since they are not members of any one team.

2. Organize the remaining students into two groups. Each group forms a side-by-side line on one side of the playing area representing a fence.

3. On the teacher's signal, two players from each end of their own sideline (i.e., fence) enter into the playing area while dribbling a soccer ball. The builders try to kick the ball away from the fence players into a space outside of the playing area.

4. After a builder kicks a player's ball away, the player quickly returns to his or her team's sideline and becomes part of the fence. All other players in the sideline move forward one space. Another player from the fence enters the playing area with a ball.

5. Action continues until all students have had one or more opportunities to dribble a ball. When this occurs, four new builders can be selected.

6. All line players should be alert since players in both sidelines rotate in very quickly.

→ Closure

Ask the students if any special movements helped players keep the ball from the construction workers for a longer time.

Names for Soccer in Various Countries

Argentina—fútbol
Australia—soccer
Brazil—football
Canada—soccer
Croatia—football
Czech Republic—fotbal
England—football
France—football
Germany—Fußball
Holland—voetbal
Iran—football
Ireland—football
Italy—football
Japan—football

New Zealand—soccer
Northern Ireland—football
Portugal—futebol
Romania—fotbal
Russia—football
Scotland—football
Serbia—fudbal
South Africa—soccer
South Korea—football
Spain—futbol
Turkey—futbol
United States—soccer
Uruguay—fútbol
Wales—football

Four Goals Futbal

PERU

→ Origin and Purpose

Games resembling soccer have been played for thousands of years. The ancient Greeks kicked an inflated goatskin ball. Soldiers in ancient China played soccer as part of their army training. The first soccer shoes worn worldwide were actually boots with steel or chrome toes to prevent injury. Four Goals Futbal (which is popular in Peru) can be played indoors with large groups of students for continuous action.

→ Activity Area

→ Equipment

Eight cones to create four goals, one to four soccer balls

→ Teaching Process

1. Organize the students into two groups (e.g., red and black). Students on each team are numbered in consecutive order, and each team has two goals to defend. One goalie is positioned inside each goal. Half of a team stays at the sides of one goal, and the other half stands at the sides of the other goal (see diagram).

2. A soccer ball is placed in the middle of the playing area.

3. The teacher calls a number, and the two students with this number attempt to score against the opponent until either one of the students scores or the teacher calls another number.

4. The teacher does not have to wait until a goal is scored to call a different number. When a new number is called, the students who were playing return to their space in line.

5. If the goalie's number is called, a teammate quickly takes over the goalie's position. A goalie may use any body part to stop or pass the ball.

6. Sideline players can pass to their teammate any balls that roll into their playing space.

7. The teacher may also call two or three numbers at a time.

8. More than one soccer ball may be used.

9. At halftime, the two groups are assigned new numbers, and the teams switch goals.

10. The students play to 8, 10, or 12 goals depending on available time.

→ Closure

Ask the students if there were any group strategies that were particularly helpful in this modified version of soccer.

Four-Team Rip Flag Challenge
NETHERLANDS

→ Origin and Purpose

Rip flag activities, very popular in the Netherlands, can be performed in limited spaces or outdoors with ample moving space. When flag football belts are not available, discarded beach balls may be cut into their colored sections and placed so that they hang 5 to 7 inches (about 13 to 18 cm) from the student's pants or back pocket. All activities reinforce the strategies used to move away from an opponent (e.g., darting, dodging, dashing, feinting, or sidestepping).

→ Activity Area

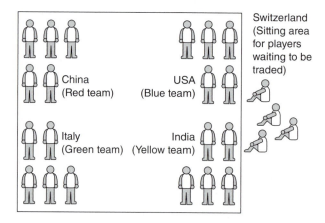

→ Equipment

Rip flags of four different colors, or strips or panels of four different colors cut from beach balls

→ Teaching Process

1. Students are divided into four groups. Each group is given a color and is situated in a different corner of the playing space. An area (e.g., Switzerland) is also designated for students to sit in after their flag is pulled.

2. On the teacher's signal, all four colors attempt to grab and remove flags from the players on the other teams. After 1 or 2 minutes, depending on the size of the playing area, the teacher signals for the action to stop.

3. Individuals whose flags are pulled sit in the designated area. The student who pulls the greatest number of flags selects students, according to the number of pulled flags, from the sitting area to join his team, and those students assume that team's flag color. For example, if a student from the blue team pulls five flags, he selects five players from the pool, who then join in and become blue players.

4. The student acquiring the next highest number of flags selects students from the sitting area to join his team and so on until all students have been selected. All groups return to their corners.

5. The teacher gives the signal for action. The process is repeated until one group has acquired all of the students and only one color remains on the playing field.

6. After the students have acquired a basic understanding of the game, have each group designate themselves as a country (e.g., the green team represents Italy, the blue team the United States, and so on).

7. Whenever possible, groups should practice dodging opponents in order to evade a flag puller.

→ Closure

Ask students to identify several sports that require players to evade an opponent.

Modified English Rounders
ENGLAND

→ Origin and Purpose

Modified rounders is an adapted version of the English game of rounders. Many sport historians believe that American baseball was a version of rounders and the popular English sport called cricket. The rules are similar to those for softball. The student at bat hits a ball into the field and uses base-running skills to run around four posts (or cones) in order to score a rounder. The fielding team tries to stop the runner's progress by catching the ball or throwing (called "slumping") to the cone or post that the runner is approaching.

→ Activity Area

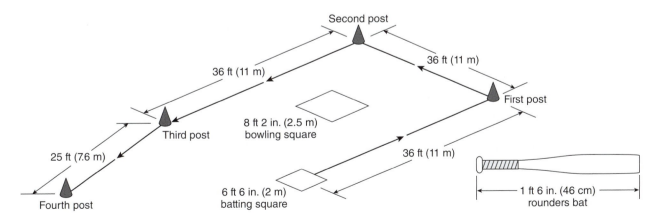

→ Equipment

One rounder's bat (or a wooden or hard plastic bat that has been short-ened to 18 in., or 46 cm), a tennis ball, four cones or posts, tape to mark the bowling and batting square

→ Teaching Process

1. Organize the students into two teams. One team is positioned in the playing field and the other is at bat.

2. The batsman (i.e., batter) may position himself anywhere within the batting square (i.e., batter's box). He is permitted to take one step over the sides of the batting square as well as the back line. He may not step over the front line. The bat is 18 inches (46 cm) long and is held in one hand. If the batter hits the ball, he attempts to run around all of the cones or posts and should stop at a base only if he is likely to be slumped. Slumping occurs when a fielder throws the ball to a cone player and the cone player catches it and makes contact with the cone before the batter can reach it.

3. The pitcher, referred to as the bowler, bowls using the underhand technique similar to that for softball. The ball must travel between the batter's head and knees, must not bounce, and must be within reach of the bat. A pitch that vio-lates any of these criteria is called a no-ball. A bowler who throws a no-ball bowls again to the same player. If two no-balls are bowled in succession, the batter automatically scores a penalty point called a half-rounder. Two no-ball pitches equals one rounder for the opposing team. (Note: One is in succession, and the second is not.)

4. When the pitch is good, the batter attempts to hit it and run around the four cones. The batter may stop at a cone rather than get tagged out. If the batter swings at the third pitch and misses, he may still attempt to run around the four cones. Therefore, it is impossible for the batter to strike out, although the catcher can throw the runner out at first base.

5. Balls not pitched into the designated batter's box area are called no-hit balls. If three no-hit balls are thrown, the batter scores a rounder. A rounder is also scored when a student runs around all of the cones and finishes at cone 4.

6. Every player on a team has a turn at bat; this series of plays is called an inning. After an inning, teams exchange roles. Teams play two innings each.

→ Closure

Ask the students if they felt less stressed knowing that a player could run to first base even if he missed the third pitch.

Finnish Baseball or Pesapallo

FINLAND

→ Origin and Purpose

The word *pesapallo* is Finnish for baseball. Lauri "Wheatstone" Pihkale introduced the game to Finland in 1922 after returning from a visit to the United States. Finnish students play the game as part of their school curriculum today, and more than 700,000 spectators watch Finnish National baseball games. Pesapallo is the national game of Finland. Using rules similar to baseball, students bat a vertically pitched ball to score runs.

→ Activity Area

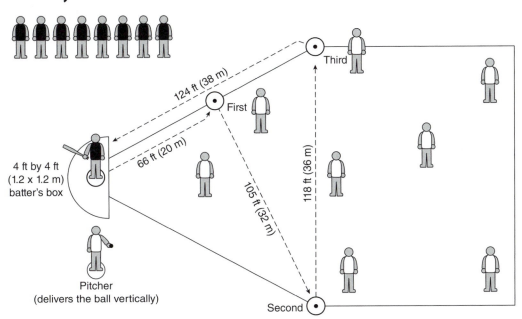

→ Equipment

Four bases, a softball, one fungo bat

→ Teaching Process

1. Teachers can choose to lay out the bases according to the regulation distance identified in the activity area or can decrease the distance between bases according to the players' abilities. For example, the distance between bases for middle school students could be 55 feet (16.8 m) from home to first, first to second, and second to third. The distance from third to fourth would be 43 feet (13 m). Explain that players do not run to home plate; they are safe after they reach the fourth base.

2. Organize the students into two teams of nine players each. Action begins after players from each team grasp the bat using the hand-over-hand method to determine which team bats first.

3. The batter stands in a 4- by 4-foot (1.2 by 1.2 m) batter's box. The pitcher stands to the right and away from the batter and tosses the ball (underhand) upward 4 to 6 feet (1.2 to 1.8 m). The batter must hit the ball on the descent.

4. On a successful hit, the batter runs into the field to the left to reach first base and then proceeds to second, third, and home. The purpose of batting is to advance runners and not simply to hit home runs. This is a game that requires extensive running.

5. The batter has three strikes. If two pitches do not fall within the batter's box, the batter goes to first base.

6. The batter is out if a fly ball, called a fly hit, is caught or if a ball is fielded to the base ahead of the runner.

7. A base runner may also be tagged or forced out at a base.

8. Each team is given three outs and four innings per game.

9. The students can be challenged to reposition their players in the outfield to accommodate the large fielding area.

→ Closure

Ask the students how difficult it was to run in an unfamiliar pathway after they hit the ball.

Comparing Baseball and Pesapallo

U.S. baseball	Pesapallo
Three bases	Three bases
Home plate diamond	Home plate round
Three strikes	Three strikes
Three outs	Three outs
Diamond pathway for running	First base in the same direction as third base
Pitching overarm	Vertical pitching
Level swing anytime	Swing on ball descent
Throwing a player out	Wounding
Can be a slow game	Faster tempo of play
Nine innings	Four innings

Modified German Fistball
GERMANY

→ **Origin and Purpose**

Fistball comes from Germany, where it was called faustball. The German word *faust* means fist. The International Fistball Association plays with a ball measuring 26 inches (66 cm) in circumference. Each team has six players, and contemporary rules reflect the sport of volleyball. The objective of this modified version is to volley and rally a large ball over a net using a striking motion.

→ **Activity Area**

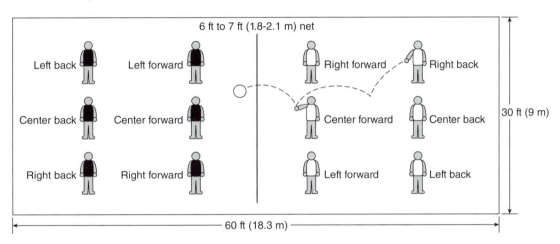

→ **Equipment**

60-inch (152 cm) cageball or a 15-inch (38 cm) floater volleyball, 6- to 7-foot (1.8 to 2.1 m) net

→ **Teaching Process**

1. The game is played by two six-player teams, although larger teams can work. The net should be between 6 and 7 feet high (1.8 to 2.1 m) to encourage active participation from all players. A contemporary 15-inch (38 cm) floater volleyball can be used if a traditional 60-inch (152 cm) cageball is not available.

2. The game begins with the right back-line player bouncing the ball on the court in such a way that a forward player can strike it with her fist over the net. Back-line players are encouraged to communicate with front-line players throughout this action.

3. If the forward-line player fails to serve the ball over the net, the action is called a side out, and the opposing team receives the serve.

4. After the ball has been served, the opposing team attempts to return the ball over the net. One bounce is allowed. If more than one bounce occurs on the opponent's side, the serving team receives the point. Each forward has an opportunity for service when her team gains service.

5. The forward-line players and the back-line players change positions after their team has scored 5 points.

6. The ball may be struck with the fist only three times by three different players (once by each player). It can bounce only once before it is returned to the challenging team.

7. Balls falling or bouncing on the boundary line are considered in play.

8. A ball served over the net may be played before it drops and bounces.

9. The defensive team may try to block the ball when the offensive team is serving. Defensive players may not, however, reach over the net or come in contact with the net in attempting to block.

10. Teams agree to play to 15 or 20 points; they also discuss ways to perform the best service techniques.

11. Large classes can play a variation called monster fistball that allows 15 or more students per team to play on an oversized court. A recreational 3- to 4-foot (.9 to 1.2 m) air-filled plastic ball can be used.

→ Closure

Ask the students which techniques were most effective when they were trying to return the ball.

Culturally Diverse Cooperative Challenges
INTERNATIONAL

→ Origin and Purpose

This activity presents 12 culturally diverse cooperative challenges that have origins (or are very well liked) in various countries. The challenges can help students develop a sense of balance, agility, and physical conditioning within a supportive atmosphere. Students work in small or large groups to solve a common problem or goal. Individuals are responsible for following and giving directions, showing sensitivity toward their peers' limitations, and taking part in the group decision-making process. Elements of trust should be emphasized.

→ Activity Area

Small or large groups scattered throughout the activity space

→ Equipment

None or very limited; see specific challenges

→ Teaching Process

1. For the first six challenges, divide the students into groups of four. The remaining challenges involve larger groups.

2. Explain that the concept of teamwork has always included everyone on a team and that the 12 cooperative challenges require teamwork.

3. Circulate throughout the playing space and use a different group of students to demonstrate each of the challenges while reinforcing the cooperative aspect needed to fulfill the task.

Challenges for Groups of Four

1. **Group Swedish sitting:** Students form a circle, grasping wrists with their arms extended. On the count of four, they assume a squatting position and lean backward so as not to lose their balance while still maintaining grasped wrists and the circle formation.

2. **Italian group tower:** Students are given a piece of chalk (or tape) and use their bodies to place a chalk mark as high as possible on the side of a wall by carefully lifting and climbing on each other's bodies.

3. **Jamaican hand–foot walk:** Students line up one behind the other in a push-up position. The last player in the line walks on his hands and feet (maintaining the push-up position) while moving forward to the front of the line. The player now at the end moves to the front in the same way and so on until the entire line of four players has moved at least three times to advance forward.

4. **Egyptian team tagalong:** The first student runs to a designated marker (a distance of 40 feet [12 m] or more) and returns to the starting line. Then the second student in line grasps the first student's waist from behind. These two students run to the designated area and return to add a third student, who grasps the waist of the second runner. Action continues until all students in the line are holding the waist of the individual in front of them and all four students have completed the run.

5. **English group balance:** The four students line up and balance on one leg while holding the ankle of the person in front of them. To help with balance, the second, third, and fourth students in line rest their free hand on the shoulder of the person in front of them. Each group must coordinate a hopping movement and advance forward 15 feet (4.6 m).

6. **Swiss toboggan ride:** The four students sit in a line with their legs in a V shape. On the teacher's signal, each student lifts her legs slightly off the floor so that the student in front can grab them. The group must find the best way to move a distance of 10 feet (3 m).

Challenges for Larger Groups

7. **English pinball wizard:** Groups of four students form a circle and grasp wrists. A fifth student stands in the middle of the small circle representing a pinball. The pinball (standing very stiffly) is carefully moved around the circle by leaning against the arms of his peers.

8. **Irish group catch:** Three sets of partners (six players) reach across each other to grasp interlocking hands to form a net while one student, standing straight with tightened muscles, falls slowly forward into the net of hands.

9. **Greek tossing circle:** This challenge uses tennis balls or small playground balls. Groups of four to six players form a circle. Each group has one ball. Slowly the students in the circle begin to move clockwise while one student tosses the ball vertically in the air to be caught by the student moving into his position. The goal is for each group to complete 8 to 10 full revolutions while moving in the circle formation without dropping the ball.

10. **U.S. four by seven:** Groups of seven students are asked to move 25 feet (7.6 m) across an area using only four or six points of contact with the floor. This requires the students to explore the best way to complete the task, since at least one of them will not be able to touch the floor.

11. **English carousel:** Groups of 10 to 12 students form a circle and grasp each other's wrists. Students count off by 1s and 2s. Slowly, the 1s lean backward while the 2s lean forward in a balanced position.

12. **Paper tag from Sweden:** One student is given a long, thin strip of paper. This individual chases other class members, who flee. When a person is tagged by the chaser, the strip of paper is torn into two halves. The student who was tagged is given one of the torn halves and becomes another chaser, cooperating to tag other classmates. The activity continues until all but one student is in the role of chaser. The last person to be tagged is the winner. This person initiates the second game with a new long strip of paper.

→ Closure

Ask the students why it was important to cooperate and assist each other in each of the activities.

Culturally Diverse Stretching and Exercise Challenges
INTERNATIONAL

→ Origin and Purpose

Many exercise and stretching activities have evolved since the early Greek Olympics when the concept of athletic competition had its roots. In the following challenges, students participate in a variety of stretching and exercise tasks originating from culturally diverse populations.

→ Activity Area

Partners and small groups scattered throughout the activity space

→ Equipment

None or very limited; see specific challenges

→ Teaching Process

1. For the first 10 challenges, divide the students into partners. The remaining challenges involve larger groups.

2. Explain that the term *exercise* refers to a series of movements or actions that are repeated for the purpose of increasing the level of a person's physical health and for greater movement efficiency.

3. Circulate throughout the playing space and use a different set of partners to demonstrate each of the stretching and exercise challenges. Reinforce the particular health-related aspect that each exercise or stretch involves.

Challenges for Partners

1. **Japanese push-ups:** To perform a judo or karate push-up, the student bends his body in an upside-down V shape, with hands and feet spread apart at least 2 feet (.6 m) and knees slightly bent. He slowly rises up on the toes, bends the elbows, and while making an upward swooping motion arches the body forward with the head up and then returns to the starting position (see photos). One student performs 10 push-ups while his partner counts to 10 in Japanese. 1 = *ichi* (itchy); 2 = *ni* (knee); 3 = *san* (sun); 4 = *shi* (she); 5 = *go* (go); 6 = *roko* (rocko); 7 = *shichi* (shi-chi); 8 = *hachi* (hat-chi); 9 = *kyu* (coo); 10 = *ju* (ju).

2. **African taia-ya-taia (tie-ya-tie):** One partner assumes the role of a chaser. The second partner stands approximately 20 feet (6 m) away. On signal, both partners balance on one foot. The chaser's goal is to tag his partner, who is trying to escape by hopping on one foot. Roles are exchanged after the first student is tagged. This is an excellent cardiovascular challenge when repeated several times.

3. **Alaskan hands and feet race:** One partner gets into push-up position, with the arms and legs straight. The objective is to move forward while maintaining this *stiff* push-up position with the body straight. The first partner performs the stunt for 5 feet (1.5 m) or until fatigued. The second partner begins from the spot where the first partner stopped. Partners take turns advancing forward for a total distance of 10 feet (3 m).

4. **U.S. triangle stretch:** Students stand approximately 4 feet (1.2 m) apart, facing their partners, and both extend their arms forward pressing palm to palm. While leaning forward, both individuals slowly step backward approximately three steps. Partners stay in this position for 5 seconds.

5. **U.S. partner push-up challenge:** Both students assume the push-up position, with arms bent and the chest close to the floor. One student places his feet with the toes down on his partner's back. The student whose feet are placed on the other student's back is in a perpendicular position to the other student. Both students push upward into a push-up position for 5 seconds. The students then exchange roles.

6. **Mexican plima:** This challenge uses foam balls. Partners stand 20 feet (6 m) apart facing each other. One student is given a foam ball to aim toward his partner. The objective is for the partner to avoid being touched by a rolled, tossed, or thrown ball by dodging, ducking, or leaping into the air. Partners exchange roles after five throws.

7. **Peru clock skipping game:** This challenge uses a 16-foot (5 m) jump rope. Two students begin the activity by swinging the rope. Other sets of partners, standing side by side, form a line facing the rope. The first set of partners runs under the rope for zero, the second set jumps once, the third set jumps twice, and so on, until 12 jumps have been completed. If any set of partners misses a jump or trips on the rope, the game starts over at zero.

8. **Swedish sawing wood:** Partners stand facing each other on any line marked on the floor. Their knees are slightly bent and their feet point toward each other. On the teacher's signal, they interlock fingers and raise their hands to chest height. Still straddling the line, they pump their arms back and forth to imitate the action of sawing wood. The object is to remain on the line while doing the sawing motion.

9. **German handshake:** Partners are face-to-face in the push-up start position. They are challenged to perform one push-up. After each push-up, they lift one hand and perform a handshake, then repeat. The point is to see how many handshakes they can perform before tiring.

10. **U.S. multiplicity stretches:** Open-ended questions or suggestions prompt partners to perform an exercise in any way they choose, and the results can be endless. For example, the teacher might challenge them to perform an exercise while bending at the waist; they might respond by touching their toes, doing a sit-up, or executing side stretches. These are examples of other questions or instructions:

   * Can you demonstrate an exercise that requires you and your partner to move your arms quickly?
   * Show me an exercise done in a sitting position.
   * Is it possible to keep your feet very still and exercise only your upper body?
   * Let's see an exercise that requires you to use both arms and legs.
   * Show me an exercise that involves twisting or turning.
   * Create an exercise that stretches the biceps.

Challenges for Groups of 8 to 12

11. **Greek group push-ups:** This challenge uses tennis balls or small playground balls. Divide the students into groups of 8 to 10. Each group forms a line, with the students standing shoulder to shoulder, and everyone assumes a push-up position. The first student in the line stands and rolls a ball under the others. That student immediately drops to a push-up position. The last person in line jumps up and stands waiting for the ball. As soon as it is retrieved, the player runs to the front of the line and rolls the ball. He or she then drops down into the push-up position at the front of the line, while the last person in the back stands up to catch the rolling ball. The action is repeated with the next person at the front of the line. Individuals in the push-up position can lower their bodies to rest while the last person with the ball is running to the front.

12. **Chinese rope kicking:** This challenge uses long jump ropes. Organize the students into groups of 8 to 12. One set of partners holds a long jump rope (12-16 feet or 3.7-5 m) so that it is 3 to 4 feet (.9 to 1.2 m) above the ground. All other students stand in a line facing the rope. The first student approaches the rope head-on and raises one leg to tap it with a single foot. After all students have had one turn, the rope is raised 3 inches (7.6 cm) higher. Individuals continue to take turns to discover how high the rope can be raised before they can no longer swing one leg up and make contact with it. Whenever this happens or when a student approaches the rope and chooses not to try, he simply bows to the rope and steps aside until one student remains who can jump up and make a successful tap.

→ Closure

Reinforce that one goal of a high-quality physical education program is for students to participate regularly in physical activity. Ask the students if they believe the notion that stretching and exercise are desired goals of people throughout the world and not just professional athletes.

Culturally Diverse Fitness Challenges
INTERNATIONAL

→ **Origin and Purpose**

Forms of physical activity challenges have existed in all cultures as a way to condition the body for greater health and physical ability. Abraham Lincoln was a wrestler before he became the president of the United States. The Asian culture used combative challenges in their martial arts training. In these culturally diverse fitness challenges, partners and small groups are asked to perform tasks involving pushing, pulling, reaction time, and strength. The word *challenge* originated in 14th-century English, meaning "inviting to a contest."

→ **Activity Area**

Partners scattered throughout the activity space

→ **Equipment**

None or very limited; see specific challenges

→ **Teaching Process**

1. Explain that partners will challenge each other's fitness level by performing tasks involving pushing, pulling, reaction time, and strength.
2. Begin the activities by having each student select a partner of similar height and body type.
3. For each activity, ask one set of partners to demonstrate the activity and then have all other partners repeat the challenge.
4. Handshakes should precede each challenge.
5. Whenever possible, reinforce the definition of the given fitness element (e.g., "The first set of challenges focuses on pushing. When we push something, we are moving something away by pressing or exerting force against it").

Challenges Involving Pushing

Push: to move something away by pressing or exerting force against it.

1. **German bulldozer:** Partners stand facing each other with their left shoulders touching (see photo). On the teacher's signal, each attempts to push the other in such a way that she steps backward.

2. **Chinese hawk:** Partners each raise their left foot and grasp it from behind with their left hand to hop on one leg. The right arm remains free but is bent at the elbow and placed behind the back. On the teacher's signal, partners enter a 6-foot (1.8 m) circle, shake hands, and begin the challenge. The object is for each partner to use her shoulder to push the other outside the circle or to force the individual to take a step.

3. **Luto de galo (loo-tah day gahlo):** This challenge uses handkerchiefs or strips of paper. In this game, which is played in Brazil and Portugal, partners try to snatch a handkerchief (a rooster's tail) from the opponent's back pocket using only one hand while hopping on one foot. Players defend their rooster tail by dodging and twisting.

Challenges Involving Pulling

Pull: to move apart by exerting force.

4. **American Indian standing hand wrestle:** Partners stand facing each other with their right feet touching and their right hands clasped. On the teacher's signal, they attempt to pull each other forward until one causes the other to lift her back foot.

Challenges Involving Reaction Time

Reaction time: the ability to respond quickly and accurately.

5. **Japanese knee touch:** Partners start by facing each other and attempt to touch or tap each other's knee before their own knee is tapped three times.

6. **Spanish foot tag:** Partners attempt to use their feet to touch the feet of the other person before their own feet are touched three times.

7. **German push-up breakdown:** Partners are face-to-face in a push-up position. The object is to cause the other person to break down by grasping the partner's arm in such a way that she cannot maintain the push-up position.

8. **English hot hands:** Partners stand facing each other. One student places her hands out in front of her body (palms facing downward). The other student places her hands behind her back. This student attempts to bring her hands around her body and slap her partner's hands. The student with her hands outstretched tries to pull them away before her partner can slap them. Each student has three attempts before the roles change.

Challenges Involving Strength

Strength: to exert force for an extended time.

9. **American Indian leg wrestling:** Partners lie on a mat side by side with their feet in opposite directions. Their right hips should be aligned. Partners interlock right arms. On the teacher's signal, the students raise their right legs until their toes touch. On a second signal, the action is repeated. On the third signal, the students hook legs and try to roll their partner over to their own side of the mat.

10. **English dragon's lair:** Use chalk or tape to mark a 5-foot (1.5 m) circle on the floor. The circle represents the dragon's lair. Partners stand on opposite sides of the lair. On signal, the players run around the circle, meet, and have 30 seconds to try to pull or push the other into the dragon's lair without having their own body enter the circle.

11. **Greek flip the turtle:** One partner lies facedown with legs and arms stretched outward in a large, wide shape to form a turtle (see photo). The second player has 30 seconds to try to move or flip the turtle onto her back.

12. **Egyptian tug-of-war:** Begin by having four players shake hands. Two players form a rope by having one player clasp his or her arms around the other's waist. The other set of players face the first set and do the same. The inside players grab hands while straddling a line on the floor. On the teacher's signal, both sets of partners try to pull the other team over the line.

→ Closure

Ask the students which of the activities presented the greatest challenge given their current level of fitness.

Culturally Diverse Race Challenges
INTERNATIONAL

→ Origin and Purpose

Many exercise specialists consider running and moving for speed the earliest form of conditioning for increased fitness. For example, foot races increased the endurance levels of the ancient Greek message runners. However, unlike the typical relay race that requires every person to participate, these culturally diverse races encourage each group to choose two or three individuals to perform the task. Each group only has one entry per race. All fitness pursuits are aimed at promoting teamwork while emphasizing strength, balance, power, or cooperative movement.

→ Activity Area

Groups of 6 to 10 students standing in lines

→ Equipment

Cones for start and finish markers; see specific challenges

→ Teaching Process

1. Divide the class into groups of 6 to 10 students. Each group decides which students will enter the event based on the key element inherent in that particular race. This factor is announced by the teacher (e.g., "The first race focuses on strength, so choose your players based on their ability to exert force for an extended time"). Each group is responsible for one entry per race that dashes to a predetermined distance and returns. Cones can be used for each group's baseline and turning line.

2. Reinforce that each line can have only one entry per race. That is, not every student is intended to perform each race. The decision on who will compete in each race is made by the group based on the type of challenge. This element increases the likelihood of excellent participation since the activities do not focus on one person but on two or three players performing the task together. To keep groups from selecting only one or two exceptional students for each race, explain that it is very important that no one individual participates in two races in a row, or that everyone must participate in at least two races.

3. Another option is to make a rule that students can perform the task to the cone and then run back to their group.

Races Emphasizing Strength

1. **English wheelbarrow** (three-student entry): Two students grasp the legs of a third student who is in a push-up position. The three students work together to move around a designated cone and return to their group.

2. **Greek rescue carry** (three-student entry): Two students stand facing each other and firmly grasp each other's wrists. A third student uses the other two students' arms as a seat. The third student's arms are positioned around the shoulders of the other two. The third student is carried around the designated cone and returned to the group.

3. **Roman crab race** (two-student entry): Two students sit one behind the other facing the designated cone. The front player leans back and grasps the second player's ankles; the second partner leans back and places his hands on the floor behind his body. On the signal, both students raise their buttocks off the floor and race to the turning line, then run back to the starting line. The front student must lift his buttocks off the floor by pushing on the partner's ankles and lifting his body upward.

Races Emphasizing Cooperative Movement

Explain that cooperative movement requires two or three students to effectively combine their movements to accomplish a task.

4. **Greek chariot race** (three-student entry): Two students standing side by side grasp their inside wrists or hands to form a chariot. A third student stands behind them and grasps their outside hands. On the teacher's signal they race around the cones at the opposite end of the activity area and return.

5. **Australian this sway and that** (two-student entry): Two students standing side by side grasp each other's waists with their inside arms and move forward by swaying right legs to the right, then left legs to the left, and so on, to the designated cone and then return to the group.

6. **New Zealand beach ball carry** (two-student entry): This race uses one beach ball or other lightweight ball for each pair of students. The two students stand back-to-back with the ball placed between their backs. Together they move around the cone, attempting not to drop the ball. If they drop the ball, they must replace it before continuing.

7. **Irish pilot race** (three-student entry): Three students lock elbows so that the two end students are running backward while the middle player faces front and pilots the trio's running path to the designated cone and back.

Races Emphasizing Balance

Reinforce that balance is the ability to maintain a sense of equilibrium while moving or remaining still.

8. **English hop to it** (two-student entry): Two students, standing beside each other, extend their inside arms around each other's shoulders so that the inside legs are side-by-side. Each student then grasps his own outside ankle using his outside arm so both students are balancing on their inside leg. The two students hop to and around the designated cone and return to their group.

9. **Italian triple hop** (three-student entry): Three students form a line one behind the other. The front student raises his left leg behind him, and the second student grasps it using his left hand. The second student repeats the action to the third. The third student raises his left leg. On the signal, they hop to the designated turning line and then return to the start.

Races Emphasizing Power

Reinforce that power usually combines speed with force to be successful.

10. **Belgian partner long jump** (two-student entry): Two students stand side by side at the start of the race. One student performs a standing long jump using the two-foot takeoff. The second student quickly moves to his partner's side and performs a second standing long jump. The two partners continue until they have jumped around the designated cone and then return to their team. A variation of this challenge, called ladder jump, is performed in England with four students.

11. **Australian kangaroo jump** (two-student entry): Two students stand side by side at the start of the race and clasp inside hands or wrists. A piece of cardboard is placed between each person's feet, so two sheets of cardboard are needed for each set of partners. On the signal, partners jump forward to the designated cone while maintaining their handgrip and keeping the cardboard between their feet.

12. **Greek engine pulling the train** (four- to five-student entry): Groups form a line at the starting line, one behind the other, holding on to the waist of the person in front of them. On the teacher's signal, groups perform two-foot jumps to a designated turning line. To increase the pace, the first player in each line becomes the engine by verbally coordinating the speed of the jumps.

→ Closure

Ask the students how important it was to distribute their talents and strengths for group success.

Japanese Group Fitness Challenges

JAPAN

→ Origin and Purpose

Literally, judo means "gentle way." Judo emerged in Japan from jujitsu, a method of unarmed combat. Judo is a formal sport, with partners (aite) bowing to each other before and after each match. These challenges allow individuals from two groups to perform physical tasks and receive points for their teams. Challengers enter a circular contest area (the ring) and participate in bouts that emphasize pushing, pulling, reaction time, or strength-related skills.

→ Activity Area

Two groups separated by a circle 16 to 20 feet (5 to 6 m) wide

→ Equipment

One set of plastic bowling pins or Indian clubs, a basketball, two rip flags or two cloth strips, chalk or tape to create a circle, gym mat 16 to 20 feet (5 to 6 m) wide

→ Teaching Process

1. Divide the students into two groups. Explain that the word *challenge* originated in 14th-century England, meaning "inviting to a contest."

2. In this activity, two groups take turns sending one challenger into the ring. Depending on who is selected by the first group, the second group makes their choice after some discussion among members.

3. Successful challengers receive 3 points for their group. This is called a *kokka*, or state of victory, and a *draw* is declared by the teacher in bouts in which the two students appear equally matched.

4. Each student should be given an opportunity to participate in at least three of the four challenges.

Challenges

1. **Japanese pin push:** Set up the wooden or plastic pins around the edge of the bout ring. To begin, one student from each group enters the ring, and the two shake hands or bow (rei). They place their hands on each other's shoulders. On the teacher's (sensei's) signal (hajime), the challengers attempt to push each other in such a way as to knock down a pin. Play continues until a student knocks down a pin by pushing it over. The winner is the student who forces the other student to knock down the pin.

2. **Japanese ball tug-of-war:** One student from each group enters the ring, and the two shake hands or bow. The teacher holds a basketball between the two. One student grasps the ball around the top and the bottom, while the other grasps it around its sides. In this position the fingers of both students are tightly clasped, and the ball should be hugged tightly. The teacher steps back and signals for the bout to begin. Both students attempt to gain possession of the ball by twisting their upper body and getting the ball out of the opponent's grip.

3. **Japanese reaction time:** One student from each group enters the ring, and the two shake hands or bow. Both students have a flag (a cloth strip) extending from their back pocket. At the beginning of the challenge they are sitting. On the teacher's signal, both students attempt to grab the other's flag and rise to a standing position before the end of a 15-second period.

4. **Japanese strength tatami:** One student from each group enters the ring, and the two shake hands or bow. Students assume a kneeling position on the gym mat (tatami). On the teacher's signal, students try to move each other off the mat before the end of a 10-second time period. *Kuzushi* means to force an opponent to lose his balance.

→ Closure

Ask the students what factors helped each group to select the player who would enter the ring.

Japanese Terminology

Sport Terms

Aite—opponent

Fusegi—defense

Hajime—instruction to begin

Jikan—time-out period

Ju—gentle

Kake—maximum power

Keikoku—warning from official

Nage—a pushing action

Randori—practice

Rei—the bow

Sensei—teacher

Tatami—mat

Body Terms

Ashi—leg/foot

Ashi-yube—toes

Atama—head

Hara—stomach

Hiza—knee

Kao—face

Kubi—neck

Morote—two hands

Tekubi—wrist

Ude—arm

Numbers

One—ichi (itchy)

Two—ni (knee)

Three—san (sun)

Four—shi (she)

Five—go (go)

Six—roko (rocko)

Seven—shichi (shi-chi)

Eight—hachi (hat-chi)

Nine—kyu (coo)

Ten—ju (ju)

Japanese Team Rock, Paper, Scissors
JAPAN

→ Origin and Purpose

Originating in Japan, this classic game has the distinction of being played by individuals or teams throughout the world. The following team approach (two-group approach) requires all students to react quickly and take chase in order to avoid becoming a member of the opposite team.

→ Activity Area

The setup for the activity includes a basketball court (if available) and a midcourt line as the center line. The two teams are on opposite sides of the center line.

→ Equipment

Large poster and markers, tape or cones for the safety line and to create a center line if none exists

➜ Teaching Process

1. Make a large poster with the basic instructions ("Rock breaks scissors, scissors cut paper, paper covers rock") and display it near the playing area for all students to see.

2. Divide the players into two teams and explain that the object of the game is for one team to have the greatest number of players.

3. Discuss the symbols used for play by demonstrating a clenched fist (the rock), extending the index and middle fingers (the scissors), and an open flat hand (the paper). Remind students that the rock beats scissors because it breaks them; scissors beat paper because they cut it, and paper beats rock because paper covers rock.

4. Ask teams to separate, form a huddle, and decide on one symbol. All players then advance to the middle of the playing area and toe the line so that teams are facing each other. One hand of each player is behind her back.

5. The teacher calls, "Rock, paper, scissors, go!" On "go," all members of both teams display their symbol in front of their bodies. All team members must display the symbol they decided on earlier. The team with the winning symbol immediately chases members of the other team, who quickly turn and retreat back to their safety line. The safety line should be identified by cones or markers on either end of the playing area as a way of protecting students from running into walls, bleachers, or outside obstacles. Players tagged before they have reached the safety line become members of the other team.

6. If both teams display the same symbol, they quickly reassemble and decide to show a different symbol or to repeat their first symbol.

7. **Extension:** In Japan, the game jan-kem-po (stone-paper-scissors) is sometimes played in a team relay formation. Runners from the two teams are positioned in opposite corners of the playing field. On the teacher's signal, the first player from each team begins to run around the square. Whenever two runners meet, they stop and say jan-kem-po. On "po" they display either a stone, paper, or scissors symbol. The winning player continues to run, and a new player from the losing player's team quickly enters the game. A losing player from either team is eliminated and stands in a designated area in front of or to the side of the end line. Play continues until all players have had the opportunity to run and all players meet an opposing player. The object is to be the team with the fewest eliminated players.

8. **Extension:** In Korea, the game kawi-pawi-po is played in the same way, but *kawi* means scissors, *pawi* means stone, and *po* means cloth. Scissors can cut cloth (scissors win), cloth can wrap up stone (cloth wins), and stones can break scissors (stone wins).

➜ Closure

Ask the students what additional sports we participate in today that are based largely on luck and chance.

SUMMARY

Having the opportunity to explore and experience sport- and fitness-related challenges from other countries is very satisfying to students who have repeatedly experienced only those sports played seasonally in the United States. In fact, one of the instructional practices appropriate for middle and high school students recognized by the National Association for Sport and Physical Education is for teachers to select activities that represent a culturally diverse environment. This book provides a large variety of activities to assist teachers in meeting that goal.

PHYSICAL ACTIVITIES OF SPECIAL INTEREST IN URBAN SETTINGS

One important goal for all physical educators is to create an environment that is inclusive and supportive of all students, regardless of race, ethnic origin, gender, and physical ability. This includes intentionally offering learning activities that have traditionally interested a culturally diverse population. The activities in this chapter are intended to address this goal by exposing students to a variety of traditional urban activities they may not have otherwise experienced. This chapter also introduces several contemporary urban physical activities that have attracted a large viewing audience on websites and Internet videos.

Freestyle Basketball Ball-Handling Skills
UNITED STATES AND URBAN SETTINGS WORLDWIDE

→ Origin and Purpose

The sport of basketball was created by James A. Naismith in 1891 in Springfield, Massachusetts, where he secured two wooden peach baskets to a gymnasium balcony to serve as targets for a thrown soccer ball. For several years a ladder was used to allow removal of the ball from the basket; then it was suggested that the bottom of the basket be cut out. The ball-handling skills discussed here would have been considered very advanced in 1891, since the game focused primarily on throwing and passing. However, the following street ball skills are very common to freestyle ball-handling routines today.

→ Activity Area

Groups of four or five students scattered throughout the playing facility

→ Equipment

At least one basketball per group

→ **Teaching Process**

1. If the number of basketballs is limited, divide the students into groups of no more than five.

2. Either the teacher or a student demonstrates the ball-handling skills for individuals to perform in their groups.

3. Distribute as many balls to the groups as are available. Encourage the students to explore and practice each skill even if they do not find success right away.

4. Remind students to keep their heads up and not look at the ball.

5. Remind students not to slap the ball but to use their fingers to dribble and control it.

Freestyle Ball-Handling Skills

1. **Around-the-waist pass:** Challenge individuals to see how quickly they can pass the ball around their waist a specified number of times. This involves moving the ball completely around the body, from front to back and then to the front again.

2. **Between the legs:** Have students standing and ask them to perform a two-hand bounce pass between their legs, then turn and catch the basketball behind their back. Challenge them to reverse the action. Repeat several times.

3. **Pockets:** Tell the students that Pockets reflects a time when basketball uniforms had large pockets to hold the players' handkerchiefs for when their hands began to sweat. Ask the students to place their basketball on their stomach at about belt level. Holding the ball with both hands, the student then releases it and strives to touch his front pants pockets and snatch the ball before it hits the ground. Next, encourage students to try touching their sides and then their back pockets before the basketball hits the ground. Students who don't have pockets should touch the parts of their shorts where pockets would be.

4. **Finger spin:** Challenge students to spin the basketball on one finger. They begin by bringing the basketball to a height near their face. They then place their dominant hand on the ball in front of their face and the other hand behind the ball. Now they twist the basketball as quickly as possible and catch it. Have them repeat this numerous times. The next action is to repeat the movement, except that this time the student tries to place his middle or index finger directly underneath the ball. Repeat several times. Most students have the ball spin on the tip palm, which is

the end of the fingertip, with the goal of spinning it on the fingernail in the seam of the basketball. If the finger is not directly underneath the ball, the ball will fall. To keep the ball spinning (since a speedy and quick rotation is required), the student begins to lightly slap it near the bottom with the tips of the fingers. Reinforce twisting the ball upward in the initial learning stage.

5. **Arm roll:** Have the students stand slightly forward and challenge them to roll the basketball up the right arm and over the neck and down the left arm. Repeat, but ask the students to immediately start to dribble the ball after it hits the floor. Practice and patience yield very positive results.

Freestyle Ball Dribbling Skills

1. **Sitting dribbling:** While in a sitting position, students are encouraged to dribble the ball around the body.

2. **Kills:** Students dribble the ball waist high, then suddenly kill the ball by dribbling it as low as possible. Have the students repeat this several times with each hand.

3. **Push-up dribble:** With their body stretched in a long push-up position, students are challenged to dribble the ball in front of the body and at both sides. Individuals must be able to continue balancing while maintaining the upside-down V shape and dribbling with one hand.

4. **One-hand crossover swing (or V-dribble):** Emphasize the need to use one hand only while crossing the ball over in front of the body. Students should go from right to left and back again. Repeat using the opposite hand. For greater success, the hand must be turned to bring the ball back to the original side. Tell the students to think of the action as dribbling and making the letter *V* in front of their body.

5. **Under the legs:** Ask the students to get into a crouched position with the right knee raised and leg forward. The student then dribbles the ball under the extended leg in a V-shaped pathway. Ask students to repeat using the opposite leg.

6. **The pound 1-2-crossover:** The student dribbles the basketball hard twice, then does a crossover as low as possible, then repeats the action with the opposite hand. The action is the same as the crossover except that the ball is dribbled twice with a pounding movement. The goal is to repeat several times and cross over as fast as possible.

7. **Figure 8:** Introduce the figure 8 without dribbling and emphasize the need to pass the ball from the right to the left hand, making a figure 8 around the legs. The student remains stationary. The ball gets passed between the legs from front to back. Afterward, the student performs the figure 8 while also dribbling and still remains in a stationary position. With this addition, the dribble pass will be between the legs. Ask the students to dribble in both directions (i.e., front-to-back and back-to-front passing between the legs). The students should begin with a high dribble and continue to practice to a low faster dribble.

8. **The crab run:** Explain that the crab run is the same as the figure 8 but it is done during walking/running and dribbling forward. Ask the students to begin walking slowly and passing the ball between their legs. At some point, add the dribbling skill. After practicing, the students can be challenged to increase their speed and quicken their pace to a running motion while passing the ball between their legs and dribbling.

9. **The spider:** The spider should be performed without dribbling while the students increase their understanding of the action. The basketball is always held in the student's hands between the legs. Students begin with two hands on the front of the ball between the legs, then move one hand behind the body and onto the back of the ball. They keep that hand on the ball, take the other hand around to the back, and place it on the ball. They repeat this same action, now going to the front. The whole cycle is repeated again and again until the action is very smooth and the students are passing the ball between their hands. The basketball is not to be dribbled at first. The pattern is right hand, left hand in front; right hand, left hand behind. When introducing the dribble, begin by having students dribble in front of the body, first with the right hand, then the left; then from behind, right hand, left hand; and repeat. The ball always stays between the legs. The action is very quick.

→ Closure

Ask the students which skills require the greatest amount of practice and what specific elements make it difficult.

Street Basketball Tricks
UNITED STATES AND URBAN SETTINGS WORLDWIDE

→ Origin and Purpose

The term *street basketball* most often refers to a series of movements specifically designed to distract an opponent in order to shoot the basketball. These tricks include getting an opponent to look away, performing a series of dodges to move around a defensive player, and performing pivots and fancy passes to a teammate in order to score. The following movements and actions may be practiced on or off a court.

→ Activity Area

Divide the class into groups of five or six students. Three on three works well for practicing the skills.

→ Equipment

One or more basketballs for every six students, masking tape to make box goals on the wall if hoops are not available

→ Teaching Process

1. Explain that street basketball tricks are used to showcase specialized ball-handling skills or can be used to evade or trick an opponent.
2. Reinforce that the term *baller* is commonly used for basketball players who have advanced ball-handling tricks.
3. Explain that the term *air ball* is commonly used when a player completes a non-traditional basketball shot. The term can also mean totally missing a shot and not touching the basket.
4. To begin, either the teacher or a student demonstrates the ball-handling skills for individuals to practice and perform in their groups.

Street Basketball Tricks

1. **Off the floor:** Challenge the students to take turns using a two-hand bounce off the basketball floor, followed by retrieving the ball and then shooting at the basket.

2. **Driving to the side:** Dribblers use this movement as a way of getting to the basket and keeping the defender in front of them. Students should practice keeping the ball low when dribbling under the opposite leg. Emphasize (a) leading with the shoulder of the dribbling hand and (b) moving the ball to the original hand and the weight to the opposite foot. This movement usually causes a defender to change his form. If this doesn't happen, the student should take the shot.

3. **The feet flip:** To perform this trick, the student bounces the basketball and then catches it (i.e., traps it) between his feet. He drops the ball so that it bounces only slightly, then locks it between his feet and jumps to flip it upward. Next he uses his feet to flip it behind his back as he jumps slightly forward. To perform the shirt catch, he flips the back of his shirt up so as to catch the ball.

4. **The tornado:** With this trick, the student approaches the defender while dribbling the ball and then palms it and pretends to pass it behind his head. He then loops it above his head by flipping his wrist and performs a body spin move (hence the name tornado) to get to the basket while the defender is still behind him.

5. **The backbreaker:** In this street ball trick, the student moves the ball from hand to hand without dribbling while staying low to the ground. He then leans back and to one side. He places the hand on that side on the ground and, still not dribbling, brings the ball behind with the other hand. He reaches his arm around and under to bounce the ball through his legs so that it comes up in front of the body.

Other basic street basketball tricks include

* bouncing the ball, dashing after it, and speed dribbling;
* throwing the ball off a wall so that it rebounds into the basket; and
* low dribbling such that the hand is virtually directly over or is on top of the basketball.

→ Closure

Ask the students to differentiate between an advanced motor skill that is performed in professional basketball and a street ball trick that is used to entertain people.

Pickup Basketball

UNITED STATES AND URBAN SETTINGS WORLDWIDE

→ Origin and Purpose

Pickup basketball is an accepted variation of formal basketball. It has its own rules and some modifications, but the skills are typical to the sport of basketball. Pickup basketball is most commonly played on school playgrounds, in community parks with an outdoor basketball court, and in community recreation gymnasiums. Many successful professional basketball players obtained additional practice by participating in pickup games. The popularity of the game has continued in the streets of most urban settings today.

→ Activity Area

Divide the class into groups of five players.

→ Equipment

One or more basketballs for every six players, masking tape to make box goals on the wall if hoops are not available

→ Teaching Process

1. Convey that urban playground basketball courts and YMCA gymnasiums have been a favorite location for street ball games. Tell the students that like any basketball lead-up game, pickup basketball has its own rules and skills. The following skills and rules are common in most courts.

2. Explain that most pickup basketball games are played to 11 points and each basket is worth 1 point. In most cases teams are required to win by at least 2 points. Any shots made from behind the 3-point line count for 2 points, while all other shots count for 1 point. The teacher or students can decide if the game will use a make it–take it rule, with a team maintaining possession of the ball after scoring a basket.

3. Remind the students that pickup basketball games have 2 to 10 players. In physical education classes, teams waiting on the sidelines can call out "next" to play the winner of the game being played. Another technique is to have players shoot free throws to determine who will be on the next team to challenge the winner. For example, five players are needed to challenge the winning team. Seven or eight students might each take a foul shot to see which five make the team.

4. Reinforce the importance of the honor system. There are no referees in pickup basketball, so students are responsible for making their own calls quickly and so that all students can hear. All students are expected to use the honor system in calling illegal contact. If a foul is called while a player is shooting, the shooting team takes a shot from the foul line.

5. Students may not push, hold, trip, hack, elbow, restrain, or charge into other students. Students should call charging (a foul that occurs when an offensive player runs into a defender who has established position); elbowing (vigorously or excessively swinging the elbows); and traveling, a floor violation that occurs when the ball handler takes too many steps without dribbling.

6. Have the students practice each of the offensive and defensive skills in small groups before starting the activity, or have each group practice and then demonstrate the strategy or skill for the class. The second method often works well with large class populations.

Offensive Skills to Practice

1. **The crossover dribble:** The student dribbles the ball across his body from one hand to the other.

2. **Driving to the basket:** The student moves rapidly toward the basket with the ball.

3. **The pivot:** The student evades a guard by planting one foot while the other foot moves in any direction. He pivots on the toe of the supporting foot. The pivot foot must remain touching the floor until the student has stopped dribbling and passes or shoots.

4. **Defensive rebound:** The student secures another's missed shot.

5. **Dunk:** A student close to the basket jumps and forcefully thrusts the ball down through the hoop. Students must not be permitted to hang on the rim of the hoop; this is considered showing off in pickup basketball and draws sneers from opposing teammates.

6. **Fake or feint:** A student with the ball moves deceptively to throw a defender off balance so that he can dribble around him. Students use their eyes, head, or any other part of the body to trick an opposing player.

7. **Squaring up:** The student positions his shoulders facing the basket as he releases the ball to shoot in order to maintain a solid balance and increase the likelihood of scoring.

8. **Pick and roll strategy:** An offensive player who has the ball uses a teammate to block or screen a defensive player who is trying to guard him. Chairs can be used as imaginary screens and can represent players who want to block someone so that he cannot drive to the basket and make a shot.

9. **High post and low post:** The high post position is an imaginary area outside either side of the foul lane at the free-throw line, or more generally, the free-throw area of the court. The low post position is an imaginary area outside either side of the foul lane close to the basket—an area in the front court, near the basket and on one side or the other of the free-throw lane, where the center player is often positioned. All students must understand these positions. Create a visual demonstration of this space for less experienced students.

Defensive Skills to Practice

1. **Leaping:** The student jumps into the air to assist in blocking a shot.
2. **Defensive stance:** The student keeps knees bent, weight evenly distributed, and hands up and in front of the body.
3. **Double team:** Two teammates join efforts in guarding a single opponent.

→ Closure

Ask students if they were surprised by the number of skills used in pickup basketball.

Pickup Basketball Terms

All day: Consistently. When a player can make a shot just about all the time, it is said that she can make it all day.

Ball handler: The player with the ball; usually the point guard at the start of a play.

Bank shot: A shot that bounces or banks the ball off the backboard at such an angle that it drops in.

Beating the defender: An offensive player's getting past an opponent who is guarding her.

Blind pass: A pass from a ball handler who does not see the receiver but is estimating where she should be.

Blocked shot: The successful deflection of a shot as a player touches part of the ball on its way to the basket, thereby preventing a score.

Blocking: The use of a defender's body position to illegally prevent an opponent's advance; the opposite of charging.

Boxing out: A player's attempt to position her body between the opponent and the basket to get rebounds and prevent the opponent from doing so.

Screen or screener: The offensive player who stands between a teammate and a defender to give the teammate the chance to take an open shot.

The Making of a Basketball

A basketball begins as a strip of uncured rubber that is cut and stitched onto a bladder. The bladder is inflated into a square shape and then baked at 350 degrees. After baking for 5 to 7 minutes under 140 pounds (64 kilograms) of pressure, a smooth black sphere emerges from the mold. The sphere is then submerged underwater to test for air leaks. Following this, 2,000 yards (1,830 m) of thread is dipped in cement so that it adheres firmly to the sphere. Once wrapped, the ball is ready for an outer skin. Rubber balls are sandwiched between two smooth, flat strips of orange rubber, put into a molded vacuum press, and baked again. When a rubber ball emerges from the mold, it has its final features—a pebbly or smooth surface and channels that can be raised or indented and wide or narrow. The ball's surface composition and the type of channel determine how well the ball will handle and its aerodynamic properties on a jump shot or a foul shot. The rubber ball is then spray painted a brighter shade of orange and decorated with any necessary decals.

After being wrapped in string, leather balls bypass the vacuum press and are sent to a table where cement is used to secure eight individual leather panels. The leather is then compressed in another mold. Leather balls are so slippery at this stage that they are shot from a machine into a cage that bounces each ball 20,000 times. The standard basketball has a 29.5-inch (75 cm) circumference, weighs 20 to 22 ounces (.57-.62 kg), and must bounce at least 49 inches (124 cm) high when dropped from 6 feet (1.8 m).

Professional basketball players prefer balls with wide channels (seams) because the seams can affect the aerodynamics of the ball, and college players tend to prefer balls with narrow channels because they are easier to handle.

U.S. Street Basketball Association

Street ball: The very name conjures up images of inner-city playgrounds, makeshift courts, and pure, raw talent—the type of talent shown only by a player who plays with an intensity, a daring, a passion that we seldom see in today's arenas. Street ball is where true grit meets true game.

For over a decade, the Street Basketball Association has pioneered the dream of street ballers around the world by merging street ball's credo of "true grit, true game" with "true entertainment and enjoyment." Whether it is played on dirt courts, in the backyard, or on the asphalt of inner-city playgrounds, the SBA's trademarked brand of street ball boasts an unmatched passion and enthusiasm for creativity that is crossing over all geographic, cultural, and economic lines. The mission is to showcase the best street and professional basketball legends center stage in an organized, competitive environment to compete, entertain, and educate. The SBA is also dedicated to discovering and introducing some of the world's greatest basketball legends. Visit the SBA's website for additional information (www.streetbasketballassociation.net).

Hotshot Hoops
UNITED STATES AND URBAN SETTINGS WORLDWIDE

→ Origin and Purpose

The original basketball was a soccer ball. This changed to a brown leather ball and then to an orange leather ball so visibility was better for both players and spectators. The original basketball players were called *cagers* because chicken wire was used to surround the courts to protect the spectators. *Hoops* is the slang term for basketball. Hotshot Hoops is played by individuals or partners who record the number of set shots needed to score a basket from various designated floor markings. It is an advanced version of the urban game known as Around the World or Around the Key.

→ Activity Area

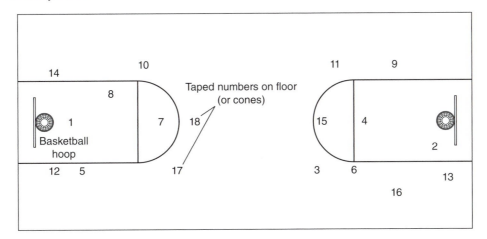

→ Equipment

One basketball court or a minimum of two basketball hoops, masking tape for floor markings, at least one ball for every four students, score sheets

Hotshot Hoops Score Sheet

Name(s) _____

Instructions

Record the number of shots needed to sink a basket for each floor marking. For example, if it takes three shots before a ball goes through the basket at spot 7, place a 3 next to hole 7. Your goal is to have the lowest score possible.

TRIAL 1		TRIAL 2		TRIAL 3	
Hole	**Score**	**Hole**	**Score**	**Hole**	**Score**
1		1		1	
2		2		2	
3		3		3	
4		4		4	
5		5		5	
6		6		6	
7		7		7	
8		8		8	
9		9		9	
10		10		10	
11		11		11	
12		12		12	
13		13		13	
14		14		14	
15		15		15	
16		16		16	
17		17		17	
18		18		18	
Total score		**Total score**		**Total score**	

Grade 7-9 Complete numbers 1-8

Grade 10 Complete numbers 1-10

Grade 11 Complete numbers 1-14

Seniors Complete all 18 spots

Complete trial 1 for all shots before moving on to trial 2.

From R.L. Clements and A. Meltzer Rady, 2012, *Urban physical education: Instructional practices and cultural activities* (Champaign, IL: Human Kinetics). Reprinted from *A multicultural approach to physical education: Proven strategies for middle and high school* by R.L. Clements and S.K. Kinzler, 2003 (Champaign, IL: Human Kinetics), 29.

→ Teaching Process

1. Explain that the original game of basketball used a soccer ball. Hotshot Hoops uses a basketball and the scoring concept of golf. Teachers will find it beneficial to conduct a practice session to review the techniques of the one- or two-hand set shot. Stress putting the same foot forward as the shooting hand and full extension of the shooting arm with the fingers and wrist completing the follow-through. The knees begin flexed, and the body completes the action in full extension.

2. Distribute score sheets to all students. Partners sharing one ball may begin shooting from any taped or chalked number on the playing floor.

3. Partners alternate shooting from the same designated spot until the shot is successful.

4. Partners record the number of shots taken to score a basket.

5. Each set of partners must finish one complete game at a time (e.g., numbers 1-18 for seniors in trial 1) before moving on to trial 2 or 3.

6. To avoid student wait time in large classes, partners make only two shots from each spot before moving to the next. If one shot goes in the basket, they receive 2 points. If both shots are successful, they receive 4 points. If no shots are good, they record a zero.

The Famous Hickory High Huskers

The 1952 Hickory High Huskers (seen in the film *Hoosiers*) were from a small town in Indiana. At that time all schools in Indiana, regardless of size, competed in one state championship. The team faced great odds against a strong team with tall, more experienced players from South Bend, Indiana. Great determination, teamwork, and heart proved vital to the small town team's great success.

→ Closure

Ask the students: Was there less pressure to score when working with a partner?

Urban Freestyle Soccer Skills
SPAIN AND URBAN SETTINGS WORLDWIDE

→ Origin and Purpose

Soccer is one of the oldest and most popular sports. The following freestyle skills became popular thanks to professional soccer players from South America and Holland who showcased their special ball-juggling skills. The Nike Sporting Goods Company began to hold freestyle tournaments in the early 1970s, which increased the activity's popularity. The combination of freestyle kicks is endless, and the goal is to combine three or more skills in succession. Master freestylers increase their overall coordination and reaction time. The most popular freestyle routines combine air and ground tricks and draw large audiences of urban viewers.

→ **Activity Area**

Groups of five or six students

→ **Equipment**

One or more soccer balls per group, lively music for motivation

→ **Teaching Process**

1. Divide the class into groups of four to eight students depending on the number of available soccer balls.

2. Explain that the purpose of the lesson is to become familiar with several different freestyle soccer kicks. Reinforce that the word *kick* in some cases is more of a smooth lift of the ball than an actual kicking movement. This factor varies with different skills.

3. Begin by having students practice balancing the ball on different body parts. Introduce the terms foot stall, back stall, head stall, knee stall, chest stall, and ankle stall. The most common balance is called the foot stall, in which the ball balances on the top of the foot in the arch area for a few seconds before being flipped off. The two next most common are the ankle stall, in which the ball balances on the flat area of the ankle with the leg turned inward and perpendicular, and the head stall, with the ball balancing on the forehead area. Encourage the students to keep the ball on the body part as long as possible.

4. Skilled students should be encouraged to demonstrate each freestyle skill and to serve as models for the less skilled students. Students should strive to perform a skill correctly at least once and then complete three, five, and more than five consecutive trials using the same skill.

5. After a student has mastered one skill, the goal is to add a second skill. Whenever possible, freestyle routines should consist of five or six different skills performed consecutively.

6. Reinforce the importance of identifying each freestyle soccer kick by name, as well as the need to practice the skills after school to become proficient.

Freestyle Soccer Skills

1. **Elastico:** Some freestylers also call this move the "flip-flap" or "the snake." It is a basic move performed by pushing the ball outside with the outside of the foot and snapping it back inside with the inside of the foot. All movements are performed with the same foot as the ball is moved away from the body and to the side with the outside of the foot, then quickly moved back in front of the body with the inside of the foot. Students should perform the skill slowly until control is more obvious.

2. **Reverse elastico:** As the name implies, this skill involves going inside with the inside of the foot, then snapping outside with the outside of the foot.

3. **Ball juggling:** This is the best known of all freestyle skills, and it is imperative for maintaining control of the ball. The key is to tap the ball so that it stays right in front of the body about 2 feet (.6 m) in the air. To juggle, students gently kick the ball up in the air with one foot and then catch it on the same foot when it comes down. Any part of the foot (e.g., instep or arch) can be used to juggle a soccer ball. The student should also try to alternate the feet, which requires a faster pace and more balance.

4. **Toe and knee juggle:** Students alternate kicking or lifting the ball on the toes and the knees (see photo).

5. **Spin:** The student begins to ball juggle but also spins around in a complete circle and then continues to juggle. The ball can bounce on the floor or ground while the student is turning.

6. **One-legged juggle:** The student juggles the soccer ball using only one foot and takes one or two steps forward while juggling.

7. **Kiss:** The ball is juggled off the toe and is raised to a level high enough that the student can lean forward as if to kiss it each time it is lifted back up.

8. **Toes:** The ball is juggled using only the toe of the shoe. The foot must point absolutely straight upward.

9. **Hot stepper:** The student taps the ball downward, using only the bottom of the foot, with enough force to keep it bouncing upward. Most students see the similarity between dribbling using the foot in soccer and dribbling using the hand in basketball.

10. **Back heel 360:** The student juggles the ball with first the toe and then the heel while turning the body a complete 360 degrees. To complete this task the student actually spins 360 degrees in a full circle in between each juggle. Speed is not necessary when students are practicing this advanced skill. They should allow the ball to bounce on the ground or floor as necessary.

11. **Outside-the-foot juggle:** The student lifts the ball up with the top side of the foot as the leg is bent and the knee and lower leg are perpendicular to the ground. The outside of the foot provides an excellent contact surface.

12. **The pancake:** Students perform the pancake by keeping the foot on the floor and stepping forward on one foot after the other. It looks as though the student is walking, but he is actually foot juggling. Each time he moves one foot forward, he uses that foot to lift or juggle the ball. The likelihood of success increases if the ball is kept close to the body and can bounce off the foot.

13. **Double pancake:** The legs are kept together and the student lifts the ball each time it falls off both feet. Some freestyle players prefer to call the skill the double-foot juggle. The ball rebounds off the tops of the feet while the feet are pressed together and the knees are bent in order to send enough force to lift the ball upward.

14. **Jester:** A jester movement involves the use of both the toe of one foot and the heel of the opposite foot. The student looks as though he is performing a rocking motion since he is kicking the ball both in front of and behind the body. To begin, the student can kick the ball in front of the body with the toe of the left foot, follow with the rocking motion, and kick it in back of the body with the heel of the right foot. Once a pattern is achieved, the rocking motion becomes more obvious.

15. **The toe bounce:** Students perform this juggle by swinging one leg over the ball and having it land on the opposite foot. The leg crosses over the ball as it hits the foot. While the students are practicing the skill, have them drop the ball with their hands onto their foot until they feel more comfortable. They can also toss the ball forward, run up to it and swing a leg over it, and kick it up and begin juggling.

16. **Around the world:** The student lifts the ball up into the air with one foot and whips the same foot around the ball in a circle formation before it lands on the ground or floor or between bounces.

17. **Shin roll:** In this skill, the ball is lifted by the toe into the air to the knee, then rolls down the leg and back to the toe. This action is repeated.

18. **Neck stall:** The ball is tossed up about 2 feet (.6 m) in the air above the student's head. The student then bends forward and ducks his head under the ball while bending at the waist. Emphasize that the students should keep looking forward, not downward. The ball must be high enough that the student can get his head under it while standing. A ball sent too high into the air will be difficult to catch because of the extra force. The ball should not bounce off the student's neck. To help make the ball balance, the student can shrug his shoulders, push his shoulder blades slightly back, and let the ball roll and settle on the neck. This creates a hole for the ball to rest in. Students can also practice the skill by bouncing the ball on the floor or ground with two hands and then bending forward to catch it on the back of the neck. The goal is then to let it roll off the neck and kick it back up in order to repeat the action.

19. **Shoulder juggle:** The student juggles the ball back and forth from one shoulder to the other. The forehead and eyes face forward while the ball moves from shoulder to shoulder.

20. **The crossover:** The student performs the crossover by tapping the ball into the air with one foot, swinging the other foot over the ball, and kicking it again with the first foot (e.g., kick the ball with the right foot, swing the left foot over, and then kick it again with the right foot). Encourage the student to keep the ball directly in front of the body.

21. **The thigh juggle:** The student juggles the ball on one thigh at a time while taking a step forward with each lift of the ball.

22. **Roulette:** This is a very basic move that begins with putting one foot on top of the ball. As the body turns in a circle around the ball, the student switches the ball to the other foot in order to successfully complete the turn.

One Secret to Soccer Success

"When players go out and train on their own, they usually do it at half speed. This kind of training is valuable, but it doesn't prepare you for competition, where you must perform at full throttle. So the trick is to schedule regular sessions of intense practice, while always leaving time to juggle and generally goof around with the ball. . . ."

—*Mia Hamm*

Mia played in the position of forward for the United States women's national soccer team and scored more international goals in her career than any other player, male or female, in the history of freestyle soccer. In 2007 she was inducted into the National Soccer Hall of Fame.

23. **Back stall:** The student kicks the ball about 20 inches (50 cm) above the head, high enough that the head can go under the ball while he is still standing. He should wait until the ball has reached its highest point and then duck his head while bending at the waist. He should look forward. If the student has executed the move properly, the ball won't bounce off the neck. To keep the ball from moving on the neck, the student shrugs his shoulders and pushes his shoulder blades back slightly. This creates an indentation, and the ball will remain steady as long as there is no movement.

24. **Ankle stall:** The student kicks the ball approximately 2 feet (.6 m) in the air and bends the ankle so that the ball falls and rests between the foot and the leg. The ball can then be kicked upward and the action repeated.

Freestyle Soccer Terms

Ground freestyle: A solo freestyle, for performance and general audiences.

Street football: This activity is practiced between two or more players who are trying to trick each other. Fancy dribbling and passing moves are encouraged.

➔ Closure

Ask the students: Which of the freestyle soccer skills would be most helpful in a game?

Urban Soccer
FRANCE AND URBAN SETTINGS WORLDWIDE

➔ Origin and Purpose

Urban soccer is reported to have had its origins in Europe, especially France. Urban soccer can be played by an individual or a group of individuals striving to score goals in objects other than regulation soccer nets. While standard field soccer is played on a large rectangular area, the urban soccer playing area can be limited and use eight objects representing goals. This activity is very popular in cities in the United States with populations recently emigrated from such places as Mexico, Central and South America, and the Caribbean.

➔ Activity Area

Divide the students into groups of six players.

➔ Equipment

Cones, two to four hula hoops, two trash cans, plastic crates, large cardboard boxes, a jump rope circle, boxes taped to walls

➔ Teaching Process

1. Explain that the objective of urban soccer is to chip shot (by kicking) a soccer ball into all eight targets. These eight stations can be created using hoops, boxes, barrels, pails, plastic crates, chairs placed upside down, cardboard boxes, taped boxes on a wall, and so on.

2. Students take turns moving throughout the gymnasium or playing field scoring goals and then moving on to the next target. Partners or small groups can also work together by taking turns and scoring a goal, then moving on to the next goal.

Key Instructional Points

* Students should advance the ball with passes using the instep of their nonkicking foot, step in the intended direction of the pass, and follow through with their kicking foot.

* When shooting, students should keep their eyes on the target, step in the direction of the target, and contact the ball with the laces portion of their shoe to achieve greatest accuracy.

* Students should stay alert with their heads up during play to avoid injury and increase safety.

* Communication and words of encouragement among teammates should be promoted.

→ Closure

Ask the students to identify the most difficult target and to explain why it was a challenge.

Urban Golf
GERMANY AND URBAN SETTINGS WORLDWIDE

→ Origin and Purpose

Urban golf is known under different names, including cross golf, city golf, and X-golf. Each country has its own history for this game. For example, in Germany the game has been attributed to a gentleman who began playing golf in a hotel hallway in the late 1990s. He was quickly escorted outside, and he continued to hit his golf balls throughout the streets of Berlin. Today, urban golfers organize events on the Internet to select dates and places where players can gather and map out urban courses. These courses include abandoned city parking lots and factories, alleys and streets free of traffic, or wherever sufficient space is available. Urban golf reflects a time when golf was played in cow pastures in the United States and players performed shots around trees and up hills.

Safety

This activity must be conducted with safety in mind. Each student should be cautioned regarding the dangers of swinging a golf club with other persons nearby. Each student should wait patiently until it is his turn to hit the ball.

→ Activity Area

Designing an urban golf course will depend on the school's location and outdoor facilities. Most urban courses are 18 holes with a par of 72, but a nine-hole course is more appropriate for school grounds. A hole might consist of a flagpole, a small wall, or a garbage can. Courses are mapped out in some city parks.

➜ Equipment

Four to six putting irons, several #7 or #9 driving irons, bucket of tennis balls (or plastic Wiffle balls with holes or low-density golf balls if affordable), bottle cap tees. Carpet squares are required for indoor play.

➜ Teaching Process

1. Explain that urban golf clubs throughout the world have very strict rules. These include respecting property, designing courses away from populated areas and pedestrians, and prohibiting vandalism and destruction.

2. The most-used golf club is the #7 or #9 iron. The #9 iron has the greatest angle and can be used to hit over an object such as a fence, a plant, or a small tree. The #7 iron is better for distance. Placing the ball on a carpet square prevents sparks if the club scrapes the ground and helps players to focus.

3. The object is to be the player with the lowest number of strokes at the completion of all nine holes.

Key Instructional Points

* For putting, students should place the ball just forward of the left toe for right-handed players.

* Before addressing the ball, students should check to see what line it needs to follow. They should keep their head down until well after the ball has been hit.

* During the putting action, the arms should be held together as a solid single unit.

* When driving, the student should focus on the back edge of the ball and should maintain this focus throughout the golf swing.

* When the club head makes contact with the ball, the right shoulder (for a right-handed player) will automatically rotate under the chin as the follow-through movement is performed. A left-handed player's left shoulder will rotate under the chin during the follow-through movement.

* The elbows remain as close together as is physically possible throughout the swing.

* For a right-handed player, the heel of the left foot stays firmly on the ground throughout the backswing movement, and the right leg remains slightly bent. The right leg is kept slightly flexed but very firm throughout the backswing. A left-handed player keeps the left leg slightly flexed but very firm throughout the backswing. The moment the club head strikes the ball, the head is in a position such that the right eye is slightly behind the ball for a right-handed player.

➜ Closure

Ask the students if this activity has sparked a greater interest in playing golf. What aspects did they like or not like?

Urban Golf Terms

Addressing the ball: The act of taking a stance and placing the club head behind the ball. If the ball moves after a student has addressed it, there is a one-stroke penalty.

Air shot: A swing of the club that fails to make contact with the ball; counted as a stroke.

Best ball: A form of team play using two-, three-, or four-person teams. The team score on each hole is the lowest score obtained by one of the team members. For example, if student A has a 5, student B has a 6, student C has a 4, and student D has a 5, the best ball and team score is a 4.

Blind: Referring to a shot that does not allow the student to see where the ball will land, such as onto an elevated green from below.

Chip: A short shot that is intended to travel through the air over a very short distance and roll the remainder of the way to the hole.

Chunk: A swing that results in the club head hitting the ground before it hits the ball, which removes a chunk of ground, called a divot.

Club face: The surface of the club head that is designed to strike the golf ball. Students should strive to hit the ball with the center of the club face to maximize distance and accuracy.

Course: A designated area of land on which golf is played through a normal progression from hole #1 to the last hole.

Fairway: The area of the course between the tee and the green that is well maintained, allowing a good lie for the ball. A clear fairway is rare in Urban Golf.

Foursome: A contest between two sides, each consisting of a pair of players; the two partners hit alternate shots on *one* ball. The first player tees off, the second player hits the second shot, the first player hits the third shot, and so on until the ball is holed. Also partners alternate their tee shots, so one member of each team always tees off on the odd holes and the other on the even holes.

Golf club: Clubs are classified as woods (including the driver), irons, wedges, and putters. A player may only use 14 clubs when competing in a golf tournament.

Green: The area of specially prepared grass around the hole, designed for putting.

Iron: Club with a flat-faced solid metal head, numbered from 1 to 9 to indicate increasing loft.

Par: An abbreviation for professional average result; standard score for a hole (defined by its length) or for the entire course (sum of the pars for all holes).

Sweet spot: The location on the club face where the optimal ball-striking results are achieved.

Swing: The movement a player makes with the club to hit the ball. A golf swing is made up of a series of complex mechanical body movements.

Tee: A small peg upon which the golf ball may be placed prior to the first stroke on a hole. In urban golf the tee could be a bottle cap, a carpet square, or an old rug.

Ten-finger grip: A grip style with all 10 fingers on the club. Also known as the baseball grip.

Wood: A type of club whose head is generally round or bulbous in shape except for the club face; so named because the head was originally made of wood, although almost all are now metal.

Modified Ultimate Frisbee

→ Origin and Purpose

Ultimate Frisbee was first played by a group of high school students in 1967 in Maplewood, New Jersey. They used the Columbia High School parking lot. This modified version is an active flying disc game that can be played with a large number of students or with small classes. The game can also be played inside. The objective is to make a goal by successfully throwing a disc to a teammate who is standing behind the goal line.

→ Activity Area

Divide the class into two groups of seven players each. The playing area is 40 by 70 yards (36.6 by 64 m) with 25-yard (23 m) end zones. The modified version can work in a gymnasium with cones used to identify the end lines.

→ Equipment

One flying disc and four cones for goals

→ Teaching Process

1. Reinforce that Ultimate Frisbee was first played by a group of high school students in Maplewood, New Jersey. Encourage students to practice the basic skills. Explain that all flying discs have specific features: the cupola (the center of the disc), the lip, and the cheek (the inside surface of the edge).

2. Explain that Ultimate Frisbee consists of two teams of seven players on a field 40 by 70 yards with 25-yard end zones. Play begins with the two groups situated on opposite sides of the playing area. One student throws a flying disc (a throw-off) to the receiving team.

3. Players on the receiving team must stand on their goal line until the disc is released. The throwing team may not touch the disc until it has been touched by the receiving team.

4. The receiving team may catch the disc or allow it to fall to the ground without touching it. The receiving team begins passing the disc to teammates. If the receiving team does not secure the disc, the throwing team has possession.

5. Play continues with the students throwing the disc down the field to a teammate who has moved behind her goal area. To score a goal, the disc must be passed at least three times on its way to crossing into the goal area. To begin, the student in possession of the disc (the thrower) may pivot on one foot while throwing the disc. The disc may be advanced in any direction by completion of a pass. The thrower has 3 seconds to throw the disc. The defender guarding the thrower (marker) counts out the stall count, for example, "One one thousand, two one thousand, three one thousand."

6. No student may run or step with the disc or hand the disc to a teammate. The disc must be thrown to a teammate.

7. The opposing team can gain possession of the disc by intercepting and catching a thrown disc or by striking a thrown disc and causing it to fall to the ground. Possession also changes if the receiving team makes contact with but does not catch the disc.

8. Each time the receiving team misses a catch on any part of the field or court, the opposing team automatically gains possession.

9. The defending team players may not guard a student closer than 3 feet (.9 m).

10. Students should be encouraged to outline an offense strategy on paper and implement the strategy on a specific team signal.

11. Play continues for four quarters. After each goal is scored, the team gaining the point performs a throw-off to the opposing team.

12. With large class sizes, try a rotational sequence (sometimes called the rotary system) that many urban classroom leaders use to ensure that all students get a turn. The teacher begins by dividing the class into two groups. It is easiest if one group lines up on one side of the playing area and the other group forms a line on the opposite side. Members of one team wear pinnies, wristbands, or tape on their shoes to clearly distinguish them from the opposing team. After every score, both teams retreat back to the end of their group's sideline. The seven players on the opposite end of the group's sideline go in and immediately start to play. The players remaining on the sideline move to leave space for the next set of players who will come off the field. The ongoing movement is almost automatic, without the students' needing to focus on their rotation, since the line is almost always moving and substitution is frequent.

13. Try a group freestyle challenge. Groups of six players perform as many innovative throws, catches, and moves as possible within a 1-minute period and are judged by other classmates.

Basic Skills

1. **The grip:** As in any sport, the proper grip is important. Stress the need to hold the disc with the thumb on top and index finger just under the rim. The middle finger is extended toward the center, with the ring finger and little finger curled back against the rim. The feet should be the same width apart as the shoulders, with the throwing side aimed at the player that the disc is being thrown to during the game.

2. **Across-the-body throw:** Begin the throw with the arm extended toward the target and roll the disc into the body as the arm is brought back. The wrist and forearm should be coiled like a spring. Keep the edge that is away from the body tilted slightly down and the edge that will go toward the target slightly raised.

3. **Backhand disc passing:** The player stands sideways to the teammate to whom she will pass the disc. She moves her arm across the body and releases the disc when it is perpendicular to the body. She follows through and points toward the person or space she is throwing toward.

4. **Forehand disc passing:** The player makes a V with the index and middle finger. These two fingers go under the disc, and the thumb is placed on top of the disc. To increase stability, the fingers should be spread apart.

5. **Disc receiving:** The receiver must keep her eyes on the disc until gaining possession. She places one hand on top of the disc and the other on the bottom. The aim is to get the body in front of or in line with the disc. When the disc is below the waist or above the chin, it is best to use the one-hand rim catch.

➔ Closure

Ask the students to identify other sports that require continuous movement.

Frolf (Urban Disc Golf)

Frolf is an urban substitute for golf when space and equipment are limited. The holes consist of four or five wastebaskets, or painter's tape can be used to outline hole shapes. The holes can be placed at the perimeter of the gymnasium or elevated on bleachers to increase difficulty. The goal is for the students to complete the holes in as few strokes (throws) as possible. As many as 20 students can play inside at one time with four students at each hole (five holes indoors) and at least one disc at each hole. The holes can be identified as par 2, 3, or 4 according to difficulty. Wherever the disc lands, the student must walk to it and throw from that spot. Eagle, birdie, par, bogey, and double bogey are all terms the students can learn to increase their understanding of golf.

Birdie: One stroke under par, par being the standard score for the hole

Bogey: One stroke over par

Double bogey: Two strokes over par

Eagle: Two strokes under par

Hole in one: Ball makes contact with the hole or object on the first try

Urban Workout

UNITED STATES AND URBAN SETTINGS WORLDWIDE

→ Origin and Purpose

The idea of using random urban items such as park benches, playground equipment, and general obstacles to move around or through to increase one's level of physical fitness became part of popular culture beginning in the early 1990s when homemade videos were first created for the Internet. The value of urban workouts is that they do not require an expensive gymnasium membership; the environment includes large structures that can serve as fitness equipment. A typical urban workout consists of a variety of push-up exercises and the use of stairs or steps, a high bar for freestyle high bar exercises, parallel bars, and a horizontal ladder, many of which are common to most park settings.

→ Activity Area

Depending on the availability of equipment, teachers can use three stations with groups of students rotating from station to station. If no equipment is available, the students can be led through the series of suggested push-up variations.

→ Equipment

Stairs or steps, a freestyle high bar, a horizontal ladder, parallel bars, and any additional available high bars as indicated

→ Teaching Process

1. Discuss the importance of using whatever equipment is available to perform urban workout exercises. Stress the need to develop a workout schedule and to pursue these exercises every day even if time is limited.

2. If stations are available, divide the students into three groups and move from station to station having different students demonstrate each exercise. These can include the following challenges.

Urban Push-Up Challenges

The American English term *push-up* was first used between 1905 and 1910 to refer to a military training activity. The British soldiers used the term *press-up*. The push-up is still greatly valued today as a way to increase definition of the chest (pectoral muscles), upper arms and shoulders (triceps as well as the deltoids), back (serratus anterior muscles), upper and medial part of the arms (coracobrachialis muscles), and abdominal muscles. Explain that depending on a person's height, weight, age, and sex, the person can burn 350 to 600 calories per hour while doing push-ups. Permit students who cannot perform a push-up to demonstrate the variations using a modified push-up or a wall push-up. The goal of urban push-up challenges is to encourage, not discourage.

1. **Modified push-up:** The student performs the push-up from the knees instead of the toes. This modification is good for students with limited body strength.

2. **Wall push-up:** Standing 2 feet (.6 m) away from a wall with hands and feet shoulder-width apart, the student leans forward to perform the push-up.

3. **Hands together push-up:** Hands are placed close together to strengthen the triceps muscles.

4. **Tri push-up:** This push-up is performed with both hands beneath the chest, the index fingers touching and forming a triangle with the thumbs.

5. **The Marine push-up:** In the push-up position, the student pushes forcefully and claps his hands together before catching the body with arms in an extended position.

6. **The SEAL push-up:** This is very similar to the Marine push-up, but the student clicks his heels and claps hands.

7. **Hands placed wide apart:** This push-up strengthens the chest muscles; the hands are placed 6 to 12 inches (15 to 30 cm) wider than the shoulders.

8. **One-arm push-up:** The student performs the push-up using one arm while the other arm is placed behind the back (see photo).

9. **Fist push-up:** This is also called the knuckle push-up and is seen as a sign that one can tolerate discomfort. It is performed on the knuckles of the hands rather than the palms. It is more difficult to accomplish than a standard push-up and is popular in Asian culture.

10. **Fingertip push-up:** This push-up requires strength, focus, and practice since the force comes from the fingers and not the entire hands.

11. **Hockey push-up:** While in the push-up position, the student brings the right knee forward and attempts to touch the opposite elbow while slightly lowering the body. Repeat using the opposite knee. (Whenever possible, use a school or park bench that students can place their hands on to perform this variation.)

12. **Guillotine push-up:** This is done from an elevated position (hands placed on an elevated platform such as steps or bleachers); the student lowers his chest, head, and neck past the plane of the hands.

13. **Maltese push-up:** The hands are positioned closer to the hips instead of the shoulders but with an extremely great distance between the hands. This variation stems from gymnastics.

14. **American College of Sports Medicine push-up:** This push-up is used to assess endurance of the upper body musculature. To begin, the student assumes a prone position with back straight, head up, and hands shoulder-width apart; he then lowers his body until his chin touches the ground or mat. The abdomen should not touch the ground.

15. **Group of four:** Each student is challenged to place his feet on the back of one person and also has another person's feet on his back. On the teacher's signal, all four students are challenged to perform one push-up together.

Stair or Step Challenge

The wild man: The student is asked to face a series of steps or stairs. He begins by leaning forward and placing both hands upward on the same step. He then uses the arms to steady the body while jumping up on another step. This exercise looks similar to a frog jump, in which the individual moves first the hands and then the feet while progressing forward. In this activity, the body is moving upward.

Freestyle High Bar Workout

The high bar is a favorite chin-up station. Students approach the bar with a forward handgrip (all four fingers over the top of the bar, thumbs around the back of the bar). They perform at least one chin-up (if possible). They then perform a straight-arm hang for 2 seconds and make another attempt at a chin-up. They should perform as many chin-ups as possible.

Horizontal Ladder Challenges

In addition to strengthening the arms and shoulders, horizontal ladder challenges also exercise the abdominal muscles. There are several stomach muscles: the transverse abdominal muscle, the rectus abdominis muscles, and the pyramidalis muscle. The abdominal muscles provide support and movement to the trunk (core) and aid in the breathing process. These muscles also serve to protect the inner organs. The abdominal muscles along with the back provide support for posture and help define an individual's form.

1. **The L shape:** To begin, the student grips two rungs on the horizontal ladder. From a hanging position, he lifts his legs to a 90-degree angle in front of his body, creating an L shape, and then returns to a straight hanging position. Each person does as many abdominal lifts as possible.

2. **Hang and swing:** The second challenge requires the student to jump upward from the ground to a hanging position on one rung of the horizontal ladder in order to hook both legs over one rung and under the next to grip the ladder. No one should remain in the hanging position for more than a minute, since having the head lower than the heart increases blood flow to the brain, which can raise blood pressure and result in light-headedness or dizziness. The student lifts his head up to the thighs and returns to a straight hanging position. The middle and lower regions of the back should be used to complete these hanging sit-ups. These exercises should be done with a partner, who spots and counts the number of sit-ups completed. The spotter stands alongside the student rather than beneath and can help him lift his head. The spotter is also there in case the student releases his grip on the bar. After the student finishes, he and his partner switch.

Parallel Bars

1. **Dips:** Parallel bars are used to practice dips as the student jumps to a front support position, holding the arms straight with legs together. The arms are in a straight-arm position supporting the entire body weight. The hands hold on to the bars with a forward grip. The arms are bent slowly to lower the body, which is kept straight, and then push up again to a front support position. Students may change the movement by pushing up to a front support position with both arms straight, then lifting both legs over together to rest on the bar on one side. Next they bring the legs back to the front support position, lift both legs to the other bar, and return again to the front support position.

2. **Bicycle:** Students may also assume the front support position and move the legs as if pedaling a bicycle. This is also an excellent abdominal workout.

Key Instructional Points

* Whenever possible, students should bring leather gloves to work on outdoor metal bars.
* Spotters should be conscientious and should observe their partners carefully.
* It is important to concentrate on contracting muscles while performing street exercises.
* Students should be aware of their personal safety when performing any urban workout activity outside of the school environment.

→ Closure

Urban workouts show students how they can perform exercises in an urban park setting. Ask the students if they can think of other activities that may be done in an urban park setting.

Urban Cardio Training

Urban cardio training takes advantage of the natural surroundings of a city to provide the student with a great cardiovascular workout. These types of workouts were an outgrowth of the training sessions developed by police SWAT teams to prepare police officers for real-life urban situations. A city environment is incredibly varied, offering a great diversity of obstacles. For the dedicated fitness professional, such training techniques enable the design of a high-level cardio workout. For example, when implementing an urban cardio session, individuals can make use of park benches, large staircases, swing sets, and outdoor tables. In addition, an urban cardio session could include any of the following activities:

* Running 1 mile (1.6 km) to the city park.
* Performing 100 jumping jacks in 3 minutes or less.
* Quickly sprinting to a schoolyard.
* Completing 25 pull-ups on pull-up bars as quickly as possible.
* Performing 25 incline push-ups using a picnic table bench.
* Running backward to the park.
* Completing 50 plyometric jumps using a park bench. Students jump off the bench and land on the ground on two feet. Immediately after landing, they spring up and leap as high as possible into the air. They should try to reduce the time spent on the ground. The emphasis is on trying not to absorb the impact of the jump and reacting as quickly as possible.
* Jogging to a large building (e.g., a museum) and climbing steps to the top and back down.

Makeshift Urban Equipment

* Use discarded bike inner tubes to substitute for stretching bands.
* Use discarded tires for high stepping drills.
* Create a weighted medicine ball by making a small incision in an old basketball, volleyball, or playground ball and using a funnel to add sand. Sew or patch the hole and then add rubber cement to the patched area.
* When making weights, substitute bags of sand, or rinse a gallon milk jug and fill with sand. Use duct tape to secure two jugs to the ends of a broomstick.
* Cut clothesline rope to make jump ropes. The following chart gives the teacher some indication of the length of the homemade jump ropes.

Jump rope length	Student height or purpose
8 feet (2.4 m)	4 feet, 10 inches to 5 feet, 4 inches (1.5-1.6 m)
9 feet (2.7 m)	5 feet, 5 inches to 6 feet (1.6-1.8 m)
10 feet (3 m)	Over 6 feet (1.8 m)
14 feet (4.3 m)	Double Dutch
16 feet (5 m)	Long rope, group tricks

Inner-City Workout: Beat Down
UNITED STATES AND URBAN SETTINGS WORLDWIDE

→ Origin and Purpose

The Greek physician Hippocrates (born about 460 B.C.) wrote, "All parts of the body which have a function if used in moderation and exercised in labors in which each is accustomed, become thereby healthy, well-developed and age more slowly; but if unused and left idle they become liable to disease, defective in growth and age quickly." In this activity, partners take their pulse and participate in a series of exercises designed to raise the pulse rate. Students record their partner's pulse after each exercise and determine which exercise has the greatest effect on the heart.

→ Activity Area

Partners scattered throughout gymnasium or playing area

→ Equipment

Stopwatches, wrist watches, or a clock with a minute hand placed for all to see, copies of worksheets

→ Teaching Process

1. Reinforce that the pulse is a key indicator of one's level of fitness. We can feel our pulse because it is actually the rhythmical throbbing of an artery caused by the regular contractions of the heart. That is, as our heart pumps blood through our body, we can feel a pulsing in some of the blood vessels that are closest to the skin's surface. These include blood vessels in our wrist, neck, and upper arm. When we count our pulse, we are determining how fast our heart is beating. A normal person's pulse rate ranges from 60 to 100 beats per minute. Explain that top athletes everywhere pay attention to their pulse before and after workouts. No special equipment is needed except for a watch that indicates seconds.

2. Ask the students to locate their pulse at the radial artery by using the tips of the index, middle, and ring fingers. They should feel for the wrist bone at the base of the thumb, then move the fingertips toward the wrist and feel for the pulse. After several trials, locating the pulse should become easier. Individuals should locate the radial pulse on both wrists.

3. Students should also locate the pulse at the carotid artery. Ask them to use the tips of the index, middle, and ring fingers and feel for the jawbone at the top of the neck. They then move the fingertips slightly down and toward the center of the neck and feel for the pulse. They should locate the carotid pulse on both sides of the neck.

4. Reinforce that we check our pulse rate by counting the beats in a set period of time to get the number of heartbeats per minute. For example, students can count the number of beats in 10 seconds and multiply by 6, count the beats in 15 seconds and multiply by 4, or count the beats in 20 seconds and multiply by 3.

5. Ask the students to complete the workout sheets. One student performs the task and the partner records the results. When the first student has completed all the tasks, the two exchange roles. Any time a student experiences dizziness during an exercise, she should stop immediately.

Beat Down Partner Worksheet

Partner 1 _____

Partner 2 _____

Instructions

1. Each student should locate his or her radial pulse and carotid pulse.

2. One person records the results while the other student performs each of the six tasks.

3. After both partners have had a turn, one partner charts his or her own results, followed by the second partner's results. Discuss your conclusions.

4. Sit quietly for 1 minute and record the pulse.

   Partner 1 _____ Partner 2 _____

5. Stand quietly for 1 minute and record the pulse.

   Partner 1 _____ Partner 2 _____

6. Jog in place for 1 minute and record the pulse. (Rest for 2 minutes to return heart rate to normal.)

   Partner 1 _____ Partner 2 _____

7. Perform two-count jumping jacks and jills for 1 minute and record the pulse. (Rest for 2 minutes.)

   Partner 1 _____ Partner 2 _____

8. Hop up and down for 1 minute and record the pulse. (Rest for 2 minutes.)

   Partner 1 _____ Partner 2 _____

9. Run vigorously in place for 1 minute and record the pulse. (Rest for 2 minutes.)

   Partner 1 _____ Partner 2 _____

10. Complete the activity by charting both partners' results on the Partner Worksheet for Charting Pulse Rate to determine the similarities and differences between their pulse rates.

From R.L. Clements and A. Meltzer Rady, 2012, *Urban physical education: Instructional practices and cultural activities* (Champaign, IL: Human Kinetics). Reprinted from *A multicultural approach to physical education: Proven strategies for middle and high school* by R.L. Clements and S.K. Kinzler, 2003 (Champaign, IL: Human Kinetics), 59.

Partner Worksheet for Charting Pulse Rate

Partner 1 _____

Partner 2 _____

Instructions

Place a dot above each activity to indicate the individual's pulse rate. After all dots have been placed, draw a line from the sitting pulse rate to the standing pulse rate and so on to complete a graph. Answer questions A and B and discuss your findings with your partner.

	• Sitting	• Standing	• Jogging	• Jumping jacks/jills	• Hopping	• Running
200						
180						
160						
140						
120						
100						
80						
60						

A. The pulse rate was the lowest after 1 minute of (which activity).

Partner 1 _____ Partner 2 _____

B. The pulse rate was the highest after 1 minute of (which activity).

Partner 1 _____ Partner 2 _____

Self-reflection question: Which activity can I use in the future to increase my level of physical activity?

From R.L. Clements and A. Meltzer Rady, 2012, *Urban physical education: Instructional practices and cultural activities* (Champaign, IL: Human Kinetics). Reprinted from *A multicultural approach to physical education: Proven strategies for middle and high school* by R.L. Clements and S.K. Kinzler, 2003 (Champaign, IL: Human Kinetics), 60.

Beats per Minute

Heart rate is the number of heartbeats per minute (bpm). Heart rate differs as the body's need to absorb more oxygen and excrete carbon dioxide changes during exercise versus resting or sleeping. All athletes monitor their heart rate to gain maximum efficiency from their training. Heart rate is measured by the pulse rate, found on the inside of the wrist (radial artery) or on either side of the neck (carotid artery). The resting heart rate is an individual's heart rate when he is not moving.

The maximum heart rate is the highest heart rate a person can safely reach through exercise and is based on a person's age. The following list shows the resting (R), average (A), and exercising (E) heart rates for different age levels.

Age 8 to 11: 70 (R), 91 (A), 130 (E)
Age 12 to 15: 70 (R), 85 (A), 115 (E)
Age 16 to 18: 60 (R), 100 (A), 150 (E)
Age 19 and older: 70 (R), 110 (A), 160 (E)
Top athletes: 40 to 60 (R), 120 (A), 180 (E)

➡ Closure

Ask the students why we are in better shape if our heart rate is slow after a vigorous workout.

Parkour
FRANCE AND URBAN SETTINGS WORLDWIDE

➡ Origin and Purpose

Parkour is a noncompetitive sport that originated in France. This activity consists of traversing urban landscapes by running, jumping, and climbing. It is accredited to French naval officer Georges Hebert, who used obstacle courses in military training. This interest stemmed from an incident that occurred in 1902 when he helped 700 people escape from the volcanic eruption of Mount Pelée. He developed the motto "être fort pour être utile" (be strong to be useful). During World War II, his teaching prompted others to use *parcours*—obstacle courses standard in military training that were later transformed into civilian fitness trails and confidence courses.

➡ Activity Area

Divide the class into groups of five to eight students.

➡ Equipment

No equipment is needed for practice. (Any obstacle that can be maneuvered using basic parkour movements, including stairs, walkways, bushes, concrete structures, light poles, or fences, can be used after the students have acquired the skills. Specialized lightweight shoes and gloves are available from sporting companies in Britain, but equipment is not required.)

Safety

Safety must be a priority during participation in parkour, since some of the moves are quite complicated. Each skill should begin with the teacher discussing safety.

→ Teaching Process

1. Explain that the movements common to parkour have appeared in action films, video games, music videos, and television action dramas as celebrities maneuver urban building structures, fences, and rails. Explain that people who are skilled in parkour possess a keen spatial awareness. In physical education classes, students run, jump, balance, climb, and move as quickly as possible as if in an emergency situation while negotiating obstacles in the most efficient way possible. The objects to be maneuvered through can be anything in the local school environment. Parkour participants are often called *traceurs* (males) and *traceuses* (females).

2. Reinforce that the primary goal in parkour is to move efficiently. Students aim to move not only as rapidly as possible but also in the most direct and efficient manner possible.

3. Stress that efficiency also involves avoiding injuries, both short- and long-term. Explain that injuries are rare because parkour is based on the control of movements, not on taking unnecessary risks.

4. Challenge the students to perform the movements slowly or in a stationary position and then increase the speed of their movements. The goal is to move in a way that helps them gain the most ground, whether escaping from or moving toward someone or something. Explain that advanced parkour techniques depend on fast redistribution of body weight and the use of momentum to perform difficult body maneuvers at speed.

5. Reinforce that each obstacle presents a unique challenge that depends on one's own body type, speed and angle of approach, and the physical makeup of the obstacle.

6. Divide the class into groups of five to eight students and challenge each group to demonstrate their specific parkour skills using whatever equipment is available.

7. Stress the need not to reduce one's momentum and interrupt the flow of a parkour routine while exploring and demonstrating the key skills.

Basic Parkour Roll and Jumps

1. **Parkour basic roll (*roulade* in French):** The roll is used to limit impact after a drop (i.e., jump) and to carry one's momentum onward. When one executes the roll, the hands, arms, and diagonal of the back contact the floor or ground. The roll is a basic move in most martial arts. To perform it, the student climbs to a height of 1 foot (.3 m) or possibly 2 feet (.6 m). She drops down (jumps) and lands with the knees bent to decrease the impact of the fall and disperse the energy safely. Upon landing, she leans the body forward toward the right shoulder and places both hands to one side of her head. This will minimize the impact to the head and protect the face. Students should roll onto the right shoulder to better protect the neck and head. Momentum should carry the student's body up with one foot on the ground and one knee on the ground. Skilled students should be able to rise without losing momentum and move on to another parkour maneuver.

2. **Parkour jumps:** Parkour jumps are used to clear whatever types of obstacles are in one's path. They can range from a generic jump over a small bush or a

short fence to jumping from a height and landing on a precise spot on the ground. Students should begin by jumping forward and upward from no height at all. Stress the need to stretch the body to its fullest extent and throw the arms forward. Ideally the jumper should tuck her knees into her chest and move her arms forward. This decreases wind resistance and keeps the limbs loose for the landing. In all jumps, the student should focus on a specific landing spot and aim for it. The eyes should be focused on that spot upon landing (atterrissage), which is on the balls of the feet with knees bent to absorb the impact (see photo). Insist that the student lean forward to transfer momentum forward and prepare for the next movement. The height of the jump should gradually increase.

3. **Parkour precision jump** *(saut de precision)*: A precision jump challenges the student to perform a static or moving jump from one space to another precise space or to another object. Experienced *traceurs* and *traceuses* perform daring and often difficult precision moves that challenge their reflexes, accuracy, and strength. Students should first practice precision jumps by jumping from a low height, 4 to 6 inches (10 to 15 cm). They jump upward and out, throwing the hands into the air above the head, so that the body forms a straight line that propels them at a roughly 45-degree angle toward the object they want to land on to be successful. While in the air the student brings the knees as high as possible into a tuck position. Midway through the jump, she angles the body downward and toward the designated spot, with the feet closer to the spot than the head. She lands on the balls of her feet, bends her knees, and swings her arms out in front of the body to absorb the force of the landing, then squats down to stabilize the body.

4. **Gap jump** *(saut de détente)*: A jump from one space to another over a gap or distance. The jump is most often followed by a parkour roll. If inside, have students practice using lines on the floor.

5. **Drop** *(saut de fond)*: A drop is a jump from some height to the ground or floor without the use of force. Some of the most dangerous maneuvers in parkour are the drops that traceurs perform from heights. If the drop is greater than the student's body height, the student should roll out of the landing. It is important to land on the balls of the feet and bend the knees, and the heels should not touch the ground during the landing. Experienced students bend the knees to a little more than a 90-degree angle, which uses the large quadriceps muscles to soften the landing. To distribute the force of the jump more evenly, the student should drop, land, and place the palms of the hands on the ground between the legs.

Parkour Balances

1. **Parkour balance *(équilibre)*:** Walking along the crest of an obstacle. Students should balance on gymnasium floor lines and sidewalk lines before height is added.

2. **Cat balance *(équilibre de chat)*:** Using the hands and both feet (i.e., quadrupedal movement) to move along the crest of an obstacle.

Parkour Vaults

Seven popular vaults with limited risk of injury can be practiced on a 3- to 4-foot (.9 to 1.2 m) solid structure that does not move.

1. **Pass vault *(passement)*:** Moving over an object using one's hands placed on the object to ease the movement over the obstacle. A pass vault could be performed over a solid object such as a large rock in a park. Running is not required to move the body over the object.

2. **Wall pass *(passe muraille)*:** Overcoming a tall structure, such as a wall, by stepping off it with enough force to propel the body forward and upward, then using the arms to climb onto and over it. Running is not required to move the body up the wall. This is also called a pop vault.

3. **Speed vault *(passement rapide)*:** Overcoming an obstacle by running up to it, swinging the legs up and over it, and placing one hand on top to right the body and continue running.

4. **Cat jump *(saut de chat)*:** This involves vaulting forward over an obstacle with the body horizontal and facedown, pushing off with the hands, and tucking the legs to bring the body back to a vertical position and ready to land.

5. **Dash vault:** The hands are used to propel the body forward at the end of a vault. The student jumps feet first over the obstacle and then pushes off with the hands. This vault can be viewed as the reverse of the saut de chat. It's one of the more useful parkour moves used to get over an object and safely back onto one's feet. It can be modified for use on objects such as park benches and short walls. To practice, students line up directly in front of the object and determine if it is low enough to vault over with a tucked jump. Using a running start, the student places both hands on the object and at the peak of the jump pushes both feet out in front of the body. It can help to push off the object forcefully and give a small kick outward with both feet. Students should keep their eyes on the landing spot and not on the obstacle or the feet. They should land on both feet at the same time and diffuse the energy of the vault by running forward a few steps until they can stop easily.

6. **Kong vault:** This vault is used to clear obstacles such as benches. It is one of the fundamental movements in parkour that rely on power and speed. Students should practice on a medium-sized object. They need to accelerate toward the obstacle and leap to start the vault, then reach out for the top of the obstacle and place both hands on it at the same time. They then push off with the arms so that the feet and legs are in a tight tuck, which will keep the shoes from grazing the obstacle. This requires arm strength. The student allows the body's momentum to carry him or her over the obstacle and into the landing and then steps out of the vault by landing on one foot first.

7. **Monkey vault:** This is very similar to the kong vault, but less speed is needed. Traceurs and traceuses jump forward and punch the ground with both feet and at the same time place both hands on top of the obstacle. The vault is completed as the legs are drawn upward beneath the body into a tucked position, followed by forcefully pushing off the obstacle with the arms.

Climb-Ups (Advanced Skills)

1. **Muscle-up or climb-up (planche):** This skill is used to get from a hanging position (wall, rail, branch, etc.) into a position in which the upper body is above the obstacle, supported by the arms. This allows the student to climb up onto the obstacle and continue. The action focuses on pulling the body upward and on extensive use of the arms. Students should practice on an obstacle that is no higher than their head.

2. **Cat leap:** Landing on the side of an obstacle in a hanging and crouched position with the hands gripping the top edge, followed by pulling one's body upward, is an advanced task that requires skill and strength. The standing cat leap is a lead-up to this advanced movement. A wall that is 1 to 2 feet (.3 to .6 m) higher than the student's head should be selected. The student uses a running-start dash toward the wall, leaps upward, and reaches for the top of the wall with both hands. It is important to place one foot as high up the wall as possible to enable higher propulsion. The student uses the other foot to assist in climbing the wall and pulls herself upward with both arms the same way cats do to climb to a greater height.

Parkour Swings

These challenges require an object to hang from.

1. **Swing (lâché):** This is a hanging drop; *lâcher* means to let go. The student hangs or swings (on a bar, a wall, a branch) and lets go to allow her to drop to the ground or to hang from another object. The term can refer to almost all hanging–swinging types of movements.

2. **Underbar (franchissement):** The underbar is a swing through a gap between obstacles, literally a crossing through or a breaking through with use of the arms.

→ Closure

Ask the students to explain differences between parkour and martial arts (e.g., martial arts is a form of training for fighting, and parkour is a form of training for fleeing).

Parkour Terms

Art du déplacement: The art of moving, used by experienced traceurs and traceuses.

Free running: A form of running that places emphasis on freedom of movement and creativity. The term is often used instead of *parkour* to explain parkour to the English-speaking world. Free running also refers to a form of urban acrobatics in which participants, known as free runners, use city and rural landscapes to perform movements through structures.

Unofficial motto: *être et durer* ("to be and to last").

Freestyle Walking

Freestyle walking is a style of walking that entails self-expression, vigorous walking movements, and interaction with one's routine surroundings. It was invented by Brian White, Brandon Kennedy, Thomas Mottier, and Mike Rempert in 1995. The sport was first demonstrated in a cafeteria at Wheaton Warrenville South High School in Wheaton, Illinois, where the sport changed from freestyle chair hopping to freestyle walking. Freestyle walking uses leaps and air moves, unusual footwork, dance, and nontraditional walking movements. Some freestyle walkers use soap shoes with grind plates that allow them to grind or slide easily along curbs, ledges, and bars. The popularity of the activity has increased, and Chicago has become recognized as the cradle of freestyle walking in the United States.

Ace, King, Queen, or Jack
IRELAND AND URBAN SETTINGS WORLDWIDE

→ Origin and Purpose

Modern court handball rules originated in Ireland in 1884. Court handball is played competitively in the United States, Australia, Mexico, Spain, and Canada. Ace, King, Queen, or Jack is an adaptation of Chinese handball made famous by Wei-Sun Cheung, who was a classroom teacher in China. Two sets of partners stand in front of a wall that has been divided into four sections. Students identify themselves as ace, king, queen, or jack. A rubber playground ball is dropped and served (handball style) into one of the four sections. The student whose wall section was involved must respond and return the ball after one bounce into a different court section.

→ Activity Area

Use masking tape to construct as many playing courts as the space allows. Each court consists of four taped wall areas that are approximately 6 feet (1.8 m) wide. Students stand 5 to 6 feet (or one body length) from the wall. The wall is referred to as the court.

→ Equipment

Several rolls of masking tape and one 6- to 8-inch (15 to 20 cm) playground ball for every four to eight players

→ Teaching Process

1. Begin by having students practice with a partner to increase their abilities to serve and hit the playground ball off the wall either for a predetermined number of consecutive hits or until individuals are at ease with the primary skills. Four students enter a court, and all players shake hands before game play.
2. Explain that service begins with the jack. The ball must bounce to the ground before hitting the wall, followed by an underhand cupped slap of the ball off the wall into any of the other three court sections.

3. The serve may not rebound off the wall lower than 3 feet (.9 m) from the floor.

4. Each time a person fails to return the ball or serves incorrectly, he is given a strike. Five strikes against a student removes him from the court. The jack continues to serve until he is given a strike, at which point the queen begins to serve. Play continues until one student remains or rules the court. All students reenter the court at this time and begin a new game, or, if necessary, four new students use the court so that everyone in the class can have a turn.

5. Depending on the initial success, individuals may substitute a smaller ball more common to handball for the playground ball.

6. **Extension:** One student drop serves and kicks the ball into one of the four sections. Other players respond by kicking the ball back into any section. This extension requires students to stand farther from the wall, although the level of difficulty is approximately the same as for the original version.

→ Closure

Ask the students if they displayed appropriate sporting behavior when they were eliminated from the court.

One-Wall Handball
ENGLAND, UNITED STATES, AND URBAN SETTINGS WORLDWIDE

→ Origin and Purpose

Handball may be the oldest game played with a ball. The word *handball* appeared in ancient Egyptian and Greek writings. In France the game is called *jeu de paume*; it is called *pelota* in Spain, where it is very popular. Today handball courts are a common element of most urban school settings and metropolitan parks. In one-wall handball, partners alternate hitting a tennis ball against a wall.

→ Activity Area

Use masking tape to create three or four handball courts on gym walls.

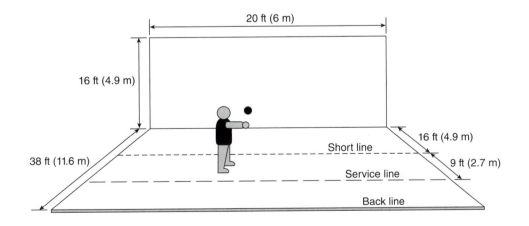

→ Equipment

Twelve tennis balls, masking tape to line courts. Students should be encouraged to bring a close-fitting protective glove to class. An ordinary winter glove that fits closely can substitute for a handball glove.

→ Teaching Process

1. Reinforce the advisability of wearing gloves while playing handball. If gloves are not available, surgical or athletic tape may be worn around the hands to prevent bruising. Partners can be asked to wrap each other's hands as a gesture of goodwill.

2. Play begins as one student stands between the short line and the service line and serves the ball by bouncing it on the floor, then hitting the ball so that it will strike the wall and rebound over the short line into the court.

3. The standard handball is made of black rubber and weighs 2.3 ounces (65 grams). Pink Spaldeens or tennis balls can be used as a substitute.

4. The server is given two trials to serve the ball into the playing area.

5. The two students continue to alternate hits.

6. A student must not interfere with her opponent's efforts at returning the ball. Blocking or pushing will result in a side-out or a penalty point. When unavoidable interference occurs, the ball should be replayed.

7. The student can score a point only when she is serving. If the server loses the point, play continues with the other student serving.

8. Individuals agree to play to 10, 15, or 20 points depending on the class size.

→ Closure

Ask the students how difficult it was not to interfere with their opponent's return of the ball.

Codeball

Codeball was invented in 1929 by Dr. William Edward Code of Chicago. He created the game for his friend, who was looking for an inexpensive game appropriate for large urban playgrounds. Codeball uses the rules and playing space of handball with a 6-inch (15 cm) inflated ball that is kicked. To begin, the server stands in back of the service line, drops the ball, and kicks it on the first or second bounce. On the rebound, the kicked ball must cross the short line before striking the floor. The opposing player (or players in doubles) may return the ball by kicking it on the fly or after the first or second bounce. No use of the hands, arms, or body is permitted. In a practice session, groups of five students can work cooperatively to perform 10 consecutive kicks off the wall. This game was popular in the 1940s and 1950s in urban alleys throughout the United States. It is perhaps best known to people who played in the streets of the Bronx in New York.

Ultimate Gaga
ISRAEL AND URBAN SETTINGS WORLDWIDE

→ Origin and Purpose

Ultimate Gaga became very popular in Israel in the 1960s. The term *gaga* means "hit" in Hebrew. The game is played in an enclosed octagonal pit formed by plastic barriers, boxes, crates, or such items as tables on their sides. It can be played in a gym, where the enclosure is formed by the students' bodies, or outside on any dry surface. Six to eight students, called strikers, enter the pit with the objective of avoiding being hit by a slapped ball that is rolled along the ground or floor. There are no teams; each person plays as an individual. Players can avoid being hit by sidestepping, moving forward, or jumping over the ball. Players strike the ball with an open hand with the aim of hitting another player. When a player is hit, she must immediately leave the pit, and another player replaces her. The action is quick, risk free, and exciting since the rotation occurs very quickly. It is also unlike traditional dodgeball, in which the ball is thrown at players with great force. It is one of the very few games originating from Israel.

→ Activity Area

To make a pit, the students form a ring. Student are assigned numbers beginning with number 1, and play begins with the teacher calling out one or more numbers, usually up to number 8. The students who are called move to the middle of the ring and become strikers.

→ Equipment

A circular playing area (pit) and a soft volleyball or foam ball for each. It is important that this game use a coated foam ball and not a hard rubber ball to avoid any possible similarities to dodgeball. (*Note:* An actual Gaga pit has a playing surface 20 feet [6 m] in diameter with 3-foot [.9 m] wall barriers.)

→ Teaching Process

1. Assign each student a number beginning with number 1. Eight students enter the pit, and the teacher begins the game by bouncing the ball. The objective is for players to slap the ball so that it makes contact with other players in the pit.

2. When a player is contacted by a rolled or slapped ball, she immediately leaves the pit, and the teacher calls another number.

3. The object is to remain inside the pit the longest.

4. The teacher may substitute strikers at any time by calling out a new number. Strikers can roll the ball or hit it with an open hand.

5. Inform the students that Gaga is commonly played in England, Australia, and the United States, as well as in most other countries with sizable Jewish communities.

Key Instructional Points

* All ring players should maintain a low position by bending their knees to reduce their size as a target and improve their position for seeing and avoiding being hit.

* Players should keep their wrist firm when making contact with the ball.

* Strikers may not pick up or scoop the ball (as opposed to just hitting it). Nor may they touch the ball a second time before it hits either another player or a wall.

* Elimination also occurs if players hit opposing players above the waist or make physical contact.

* Encourage students to avoid "Gaga knuckle." This common injury occurs when a player's knuckles scrape against the playing surface as she attempts to hit the ball. Students in Israel often wrap tube socks on their hands to prevent injury.

→ Closure

Ask what strategy worked best for the players in the role of strikers and have students explain why that strategy was successful.

Blister

→ Origin and Purpose

Blister is a highly active urban throwing game that allows members of two teams to use three or four balls to knock an oversized ball through the opposing team's goal. Players can throw only their own colored balls and may not interfere with the other team's balls. The game takes its name from the hours of play (and blisters on the hands) associated with the ongoing challenge. Many cities claim that Blister originated in urban streets among older students when throwing smaller balls or rocks at a basketball or in connection with angle shots for pool (i.e., billiards).

→ Activity Area

Divide the class into two groups of 8 to 10 players depending on the size of the playing area. Each group is given three or four playground balls of one color to hold in their possession. The oversized ball is placed in the middle of the playing area.

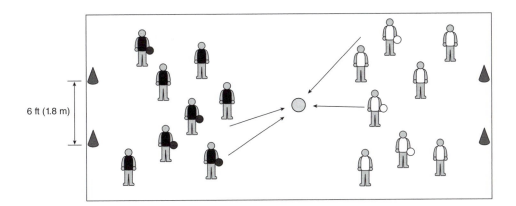

6 ft (1.8 m)

→ Equipment

One oversized rubber playground ball (at least 16 inches [40 cm] in diameter); three or four playground balls (6 to 8 inches [15 to 20 cm] in diameter) or heavy foam balls all of the same color for each team; masking tape to stripe one team's balls if necessary; four cones to create two 6-foot (1.8 m) goals on opposite sides of the playing field. If equipment is limited, the game can also be played using one oversized ball and two marked soccer balls.

→ Teaching Process

1. Reinforce that the object of the game is to cooperate with one's teammates to direct an oversized ball called the "play ball" through the goal. No player is allowed to touch the play ball in any way.

2. Explain that each team has three or four balls to manipulate and throw at the play ball. These balls are called bump balls. By working as a team, players try to drive the play ball into the opponent's goal.

3. Players can retrieve only their own bump balls, and the play ball can be moved only by a thrown bump ball.

4. There is no goalie in this game, although a bump ball can be thrown at any time to a teammate who is in a better position to move the play ball into the goal.

5. After each score, a new group of students goes in to play.

→ Closure

Ask the students: How much of an advantage was it to have teammates scattered throughout the playing area?

Square Four
CANADA AND URBAN SETTINGS WORLDWIDE

→ Origin and Purpose

The English play numerous games involving boxes or squares painted on the ground. The game of Square Four (also called Four Square) is common to schools and recreational settings worldwide. Lines scratched into the dirt or painted on asphalt surfaces replaced the need for the one- and four-way courts commonly used in handball. In this activity, one student serves a 6- to 10-inch (15 to 25 cm) playground ball into an opponent's box. The student receiving the ball must return the serve into one of three boxes in the playing area. Action continues until the ball is not properly returned into a box.

→ Activity Area

Students are divided according to the number of Square Four diagrams the space allows.

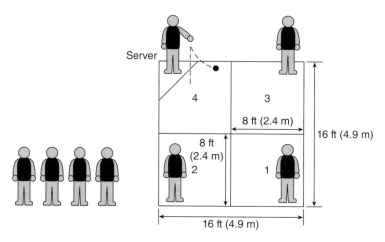

→ Equipment

Masking tape or chalk to create squares, one rubber playground ball (preferably 8 inches, or 20 cm) for each square

→ Teaching Process

1. Explain that some adults call this activity Four Square, which in recent years has become the more common name. In some urban settings the activity is known as boxball. Tell students that in order to become a Four Square world champion, 15- to 17-year-old contestants need daily training, must learn advanced serving strategies, and must beat out as many as 40 players in a tournament. To begin the activity, students conduct a practice session by hitting a playground ball back and forth, underhand, with open palms.

2. Four students position themselves at the outside corner of the playing boxes. The student in box 4 is the server and begins the action by saying, "Ready." The server then drops the ball into the back corner of his box (called the mailbox) and, after the ball bounces once, taps it (underhand with open palms) into box 1.

3. The serve must always go to box 1 and must be returnable (i.e., not too high, fast, or forceful). Explain to students that the phrase "no blood on serves" has helped to instill fair play for many years.

4. The box 1 player responds to the serve by returning the ball with an underhand tap so that it falls into another student's box. The ball may not be caught or held but should be returned using one or two open palms.

5. Action continues until a student fails to return the ball into a box.

6. When a student is not able to return the serve, he moves to the end of the waiting line. The other players, with the exception of the server, move to the next numbered box.

7. The objective is to remain or become the server in box 4.

8. Balls falling on the lines should be played. Overhand smashes are not permitted.

9. Returning the ball by striking it with a closed fist is not allowed.

10. There are two forms of scoring. Players can simply try to maintain the role of server and stay in the game. A formal scoring system has been designed for national championships, which are conducted every year on the East Coast. A player's success and prize money are calculated and the trophy is awarded according to these three criteria:

    * ENT: The total number of times a student has entered the court and played a game.

    * SRV: The total number of times a player has served the ball.

    * AVG: The cumulative ratio of SRV to ENT (i.e., number of times as server divided by number of games played) in a tournament.

Practice Game Variations

1. **Around the Horn:** The server calls out, "Ready," followed by "Around the horn." The serve must be placed to the server's right or left and must be hit in order from box

---

International Four Square Rule Difference

The basic court measures 20 by 20 feet (6 by 6 m). It is divided into fourths to make four 10- by 10-foot (3 by 3 m) squares. A 40-square-foot (12 square m) square is drawn around the court (creating the spike zone). In this variation, after a player returns a serve or a ball hit into his box, the ball may not bounce outside the spike zone; if it does, the player has hit the ball too hard and it is out. The player is out, a new player enters box 1, and the ball is returned to the server in box 4.

to box until it returns to the server. This action continues until the server regains the ball or calls out a different variation.

2. **Challenge:** The server calls out, "Ready," followed by "Challenge." The server may serve to any student, but the ball must be returned to the server until the server calls out, "End of challenge." Each time a player receives the ball, he must hit it back to the server.

3. **Duel:** The server calls out, "Ready," followed by "Duel." The serve can be placed to any of the other three players. The student receiving the serve must hit the ball back to the server, and the action continues between those two players until the server says, "End of duel."

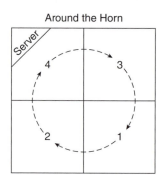
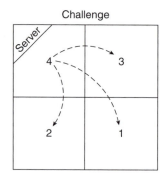
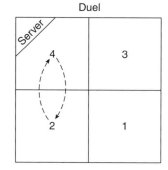

➔ **Closure**

Ask the students how difficult it was to control their disappointment or anger when they failed to return a ball.

Stickball

ENGLAND AND URBAN SETTINGS WORLDWIDE

➔ **Origin and Purpose**

The game of stickball originated in England during the 18th century. Batters may choose to self-hit or fungo hit (that is, to bat after tossing the ball into the air), to receive an overhand pitch that bounces once before reaching the plate, or to receive a regular underhand or overhand pitch to increase the opportunities for success.

➔ **Activity Area**

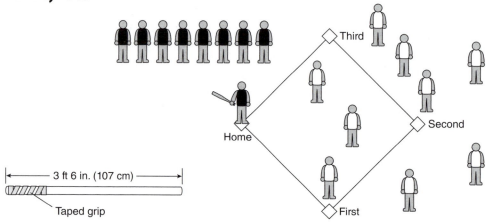

→ **Equipment**

Stickball bat, pink Spaldeens or tennis balls

→ **Teaching Process**

1. Play begins with the class divided into two teams. First, second, and third base and home plate may be designated with chalk, regulation softball bags, gymnasium cones, or even things like the markings on a side of a building.

2. Pink Spaldeens and tennis balls are most commonly used. Balls may be cut in half when the size of the playing area is limited.

3. The game begins with a student from each team following the old custom of grasping the bat hand-over-hand. The student whose hand ends up nearest the top of the bat chooses to have her team bat or take the field.

4. Students assume playing positions as in softball or baseball.

5. Individuals at bat can decide to fungo hit, receive a pitched ball that bounces at least once before reaching the batting area, or receive a regular underhand or overhand pitch. Three strikes and three outs apply, with as many innings as time permits.

6. When a player decides to perform a fungo hit, the teacher should stress the need to toss the ball upward, let it bounce once, and then swing.

7. No balls or fouls are called in this game.

8. Whenever possible, students hitting home runs should be given the opportunity to carve or write their initials on the bat.

→ **Closure**

Ask the students to identify and discuss the pros and cons of using different batting techniques.

Three-Team Softball
UNITED STATES

→ **Origin and Purpose**

Softball was intended as a winter substitute for baseball. In 1908, the National Amateur Playground Ball Association was formed, and the organization promoted the idea of playing the game outdoors. This activity works very well in urban settings because it can accommodate large or small classes and eliminates the situation in which one team loses. It also increases the likelihood that more students will have turns at bat before three outs occur.

→ **Activity Area**

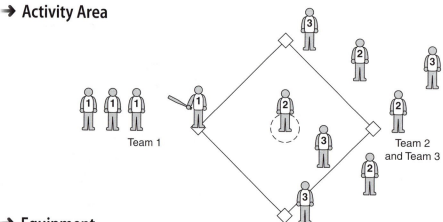

Team 1

Team 2
and Team 3

→ **Equipment**

One to three softballs and a softball bat

→ **Teaching Process**

1. Explain that the English word *team* stems from the Latin word *ducere*, meaning to pull together. Divide the students into three groups or teams (i.e., teams 1, 2, and 3).

2. Teams 2 and 3 work together performing fielding positions while team 1 bats.

3. After team 1 has made three outs or every student on the team has had a turn at bat, team 2 is given the opportunity to bat, followed by team 3.

4. Stress the need for groups in the field to reposition players for effective defense.

5. General softball rules apply.

6. Pique the students' interest by stressing that a baseball home plate is actually an irregular pentagon. The front measures 17 inches (43 cm). The parallel sides measure 8.5 inches (22 cm), and these lines connect to the foul lines. The tip consists of 12-inch (30 cm) sides that meet at a point.

Balls-Deep Urban Softball

Balls deep is a phrase that students might use when playing softball with great intensity. Students sometimes use the phrase to signify something that is overwhelming, irresistible, or powerful. This is an urban term that teachers should be aware of but not use.

→ **Closure**

Ask the students if teams were able to work collaboratively while in the field.

Chicago Baseball: An Urban Activity at Its Best

The city of Chicago, where softball originated, is also known for its own version of softball, which uses a 16-inch (40 cm) DeBeer Clincher Softball. This variation of softball is great for urban physical education classes because it uses a large, heavy softball and a lob underhand pitch and does not require gloves. The size of the ball increases the likelihood of batting; but the weight of the ball also means that most of the action takes place in the infield, so students do not spend their class time chasing a hit ball. All that is needed is one ball and a bat.

Ultimate Keep Away
UNITED STATES AND URBAN SETTINGS WORLDWIDE

→ Origin and Purpose

The world's four most popular sports (i.e., football, soccer, baseball/softball, and basketball) are different because of the type of ball used and the type of motor skill required to move the ball forward or complete a pass. In this activity, two groups of students use a variety of balls, and teams try to complete a predetermined number of consecutive passes before the opposition can do so.

→ Activity Area

Divide the students into groups of six to eight players. Any standard gymnasium or outdoor playing space can work for this activity.

→ Equipment

One basketball, one football, one soccer ball, and one softball or baseball; pinnies, jerseys, or wristbands to distinguish players on two teams

→ Teaching Process

1. Students are organized into two teams of six to eight players. The game begins with the teacher tossing up one of the four balls between two opposing students in the center of the playing area.

2. Whichever team gains possession of the toss begins passing the ball in the appropriate manner (i.e., soccer instep kick, basketball chest or bounce pass, football forward pass, softball overhead throw).

3. Each time a player receives a pass, he calls out a number (i.e., the first person to receive calls out the number 1, the second calls out the number 2, and so on).

4. The opponents try to intercept the ball and begin their own series of consecutive passes.

5. Both teams must decide on a magic number to reach with a particular ball before the teacher tosses up the next ball for play. Teams may decide, for example, to play for five consecutive passes with the soccer ball and 10 passes with the softball.

6. Students should be encouraged to use a clipboard, paper, and marker to draw the positions and running patterns for the greatest likelihood of consecutive passes.

→ Closure

Ask the students whether each team conceded gracefully when the opponent was successful and which game strategy was most effective.

The Harlem Shake
UNITED STATES

→ Origin and Purpose

The Harlem Shake originated in the 1980s in Harlem, in New York City. The dance is based on an East African dance called Eskista, and it is believed that early African immigrants contributed to its development.

→ Activity Area

Students are scattered throughout the activity area, with sufficient space between them to enable free and open dance movements.

→ Equipment

Hip-hop music, CD player or other music player with speakers

→ Teaching Process

1. Ask the students to keep their feet at shoulder width and to place their arms at the sides of the body.

2. Each student brings her left shoulder upward and then downward while pushing her hips out to the right. The torso should be kept still.

3. Next, the action is repeated in reverse (i.e., the right shoulder is pushed upward and then downward while the hips are moved to the left). It is important to keep the dance movements in sync.

4. Students repeat these two movements to the beat of the music until a flowing action becomes dominant.

5. At some point, have students add the shimmy shake movement—bending forward and shaking the shoulders back and forth in small, quick movements. Students should be encouraged to change speeds as they perform the shimmy shake.

6. To initiate the foot movements, challenge the students to stand with their feet parallel. Have them move the toe of the right foot to the right while moving the heel of the left foot to the right at the same time. Then they move the heel of the right foot to the right while moving the toe of the left foot to the right. Continue the sequence while adding the shoulder movements.

Key Instructional Points

* Students should bend the body forward while shimmying.
* Arms should be kept close to the body.
* Students should concentrate on moving to the beat of the music.

→ Closure

Ask: Did the music help or hinder your coordination when you were performing the dance?

Krumping

UNITED STATES

→ Origin and Purpose

Krumping is characterized by free, expressive, and highly energetic upper torso movements. It originated in the early 1990s in South Central Los Angeles, where it was used as a way to dance and entertain others and focus on rising above socioeconomic hardships such as poverty, crime, and violence. The term *krumping* comes from the acronym KRUMP, which stands for kingdom of radically uplifted mighty praise. The positive energy released with krumping is aimed at showing off superior dance skills to competing groups of dancers. Krumping has evolved into a major dance movement in hip-hop because of its fast pace and sharp upper torso moves.

→ Activity Area

Students are scattered throughout the activity area, with sufficient space between them to enable free and open dance movements.

→ Equipment

Hip-hop music, CD player or other music player with speakers

→ Teaching Process

1. Explain to the students that krumping has three main components: the stomp, the chest pop, and arm swings.

2. If we view a krump dance like a sentence, the stomp is the beginning of the sentence. The stomp is the movement that one makes with the legs to start the dance. It is an emphatic or explosive step in which most often the toe grinds into the floor. Dancers often use three expressive stomps.

3. The second part of the dance is the chest pop. The chest pop can be thought of as an explosion that comes from within the center of the body. To chest pop, the student assumes a wide stance with an easy form. He begins by pushing out the chest and then quickly brings it in (down). It looks like snapping the chest out and then snapping it in. Students should make this move easily and simply.

4. The third part of krumping is arm swings. The arm swings, which may include making a fist, involve movements from the center of the body outward or movements upward or downward.

5. In krumping the dancer displays an attitude—confident, goofy, foolish, funny, or rugged, for example. Ask the students to think about what attitude they want to display when dancing.

6. Thrusting movements are also an aspect of the krump. Encourage the students to begin by planting their feet shoulder-width apart. Have them place their hands under the chin area with their thumbs pointing downward and the fingertips nearly touching. The elbows are out to the sides of the body.

7. Students thrust the top part of the body forward as if they were lunging for someone. They complete this move by simultaneously pushing both the arms and hips forward. The thrusting movement is aggressive and forceful.

8. Next, the students pull their torso back as if someone were lunging toward them. This movement should reflect a strong emotion. All students bring their arms back to the body and bring their hips back at the same time.

9. Extend the dance by asking the students to improvise and create their own movements. Have them stomp their feet or move about and expand their chests to express power.

10. Challenge partners to create and experiment with different moves.

11. Taunting precedes the dance itself. Taunts are a way of psyching or intimidating competing dancers before someone begins krumping.

Key Instructional Points

* All movements should be very distinctive.
* Students should concentrate on moving to the beat of the music.
* They should keep their focus on their attitude while dancing.

→ Closure

Krumping encourages dancers to display an attitude. Ask, "Were you satisfied that your dance expressed your feeling of who you are?"

Krumping Terms

Character: An emotion or attitude portrayed in the dance (e.g., a humorous or funny character).

Power moves: Swinging of arms in a powerful, forceful motion; stomping one's feet; powerful chest pops.

Sync moves: Simultaneous movements of the arms and legs (e.g., crossing arms and legs at the same time).

Taunt: A means of psyching or intimidating competing dancers before one begins krumping.

Traveling: The manner in which the student moves from place to place during the dance.

Tricks: Techniques that dancers use during the dance to give themselves an opportunity to rest or to catch their breath. These may involve several moves grouped together.

SUMMARY

While implementing the activities presented in this chapter, it is important to reflect on their origins. Hopefully the students not only experience and appreciate several new physical skills but also acquire historical facts about the games and how they were developed. This newly learned information may spark a stronger interest in cultural activities and an appreciation for differences. The skills described in the chapter, as well as many of the activities, are quite challenging and in many cases likely to be unfamiliar. They should give individuals an opportunity to demonstrate advanced motor skills to their peers, which in turn may bring praise to the student who might not otherwise receive any recognition. Perhaps the most important element of these activities is the novelty factor, which can appeal to all students and especially those in urban settings.

CHAPTER 5

ASSESSING DIVERSITY OUTCOMES

Rubrics have become an invaluable form of assessment in all aspects of today's educational system. Rubrics contain specific criteria for assessing student performance. Numerical scores are often given to levels of achievement, followed by a summary score for the overall performance. The scores for all the criteria are added together to establish this summary score. The rubric often includes space for the teacher to explain the rationale for each judgment or make suggestions for the student or groups of students being assessed. Rubrics provide a clear and multidimensional explanation for the numerical score given to a student's performance or interaction or simply indicate how successful the teacher was in meeting the lesson's objectives.

This chapter includes four sample rubrics:

* Rubric 1: Preparing Physical Education Candidates to Teach in Diverse Settings
* Rubric 2: Assessing Individual Interaction With a Partner or Peer
* Rubric 3: Assessing a Student's Group Interactive Skills
* Rubric 4: Assessing the Extent to Which Objectives Have Been Achieved in a Class

Rubric 1 can be used in a physical education teacher education program. It is aimed at assessing the extent to which preservice candidates are prepared to teach in a diverse physical education setting. It is essential that teacher candidates enter the profession knowing how to work successfully in a diverse setting. With the growing numbers of different cultures in our schools, future teachers should be comfortable with a variety of practices to address the needs of these populations. This first rubric can be used to assess the extent to which a teacher training program conveys information regarding diversity.

Rubric 2 focuses on the student's individual interaction with a partner or peer. This rubric is used by the physical education teacher to appraise the extent of positive socialization that one student experiences while working with another. The extent of interaction ranges from a low of 1 point, indicating that the teacher needed to prompt or ask the student to interact with a classmate, to 4 points, representing excellent interaction. The scores of the rubric may reflect that some students will achieve a perfect score of 40 points while others need intervention.

Using rubric 3, the teacher observes one student's performance throughout a lesson and uses the descriptors to determine the student's success in socializing, mingling, and cooperating with small or large groups of peers. As with rubric 2, the student can achieve 40 points by always exhibiting the willingness and effort to participate wholeheartedly in the activities. This rubric assesses a student's ability to work within a group. This assessment may represent the success or failure of an individual to make it as a member of a team.

Rubric 4 differs from the other three in that it focuses on the extent to which teachers feel that they accomplished the objectives of a lesson. The rubric affords the teacher a specific way to evaluate the success of the class. Teachers may use and adjust this rubric to evaluate the objectives in the cognitive, psychomotor, or affective domain or more than one of these domains. They may administer the rubric immediately after lesson closure or during self-reflection time. On the basis of the results, they can decide to repeat the activity with future classes or to expand or modify the content to better meet their initial objectives.

Student journals can also be used to collect data on the progress of student learning. Information collected from journals reveals the individual's perceptions and feelings about participating in the physical activity. Students should be asked to record their feelings at regular intervals. Although ranging in depth of self-reflection, the information provides results that are not evident through observation. The information can be recorded on index cards if journals are not available. The results compiled from journals can be used at the end of each school's ranking period for a summary analysis.

Sample Rubric 1:
Preparing Physical Education Candidates to Teach in Diverse Settings

Name: _____ Date: _____

Course number: _____ Course title: _____

Additional: _____

Examples of Forms of Evidence

- Name of a specific assignment related to this issue or topic
- Unit plan and content information project related to multicultural games and other physical activity content
- Analysis of video *Teaching Tolerance*
- Completed lesson plans that focus on cultural differences and similarities (e.g., international sports)
- Discussions of socioeconomic considerations

Circle Yes or No to indicate if the behavior or performance has been demonstrated and cite evidence used to make this determination.

Candidates are provided with a well-grounded framework for understanding diversity, including English language learners and students with exceptionalities.	Yes No Supportive evidence:
Candidates appropriately adapt instruction for services for all students, including linguistically and culturally diverse students and students with exceptionalities.	Yes No Supportive evidence:
Candidates intentionally select activities and challenges that reflect a culturally diverse environment.	Yes No Supportive evidence:
Candidates communicate with students and families in ways that demonstrate sensitivity to cultural and gender differences.	Yes No Supportive evidence:
Candidates are aware of common protocols used for teaching large classes and advanced management techniques to address triggers that might promote class concerns.	Yes No Supportive evidence:
Candidates identify ways to enhance the school climate and value diversity (e.g., themed bulletin boards, photos, posters of athletes participating in physical activity, charts or records of student accomplishments).	Yes No Supportive evidence:
Candidates demonstrate behaviors that are consistent with the ideas of fairness and the belief that all students can learn.	Yes No Supportive evidence:
Candidate proficiencies related to diversity are assessed, and the data are used to provide feedback to candidates for improving their knowledge, skills, and professional dispositions for helping students from diverse populations to learn.	Yes No Supportive evidence:

From R.L. Clements and A. Meltzer Rady, 2012, *Urban physical education: Instructional practices and cultural activities* (Champaign, IL: Human Kinetics).

Sample Rubric 2:
Assessing Individual Interaction
With a Partner or Peer

Teacher's name: _____

Student's name: _____

Class period: _____ Grade: _____ Date: _____

Circle each appropriate score.

	4 Excellent interaction *Always*	3 Good interaction *Usually*	2 Somewhat interactive *Sometimes*	1 Poor interaction *Needs to be asked or does not exhibit appropriate behavior*
The student's willingness to practice with a partner	4	3	2	1
The student's willingness to encourage a partner to verbalize his or her opinion	4	3	2	1
The student's willingness to respond to a partner without ridiculing his or her ideas	4	3	2	1
The student's willingness to be tolerant of a partner's limitations	4	3	2	1
The student's willingness to be attentive to a partner's questions	4	3	2	1
The student's willingness to assist his or her partner in the organization and execution of the activity	4	3	2	1
The student's willingness to accommodate a partner's needs	4	3	2	1
The student's willingness to offer praise when appropriate	4	3	2	1
The student's willingness to demonstrate cooperative gestures with a partner	4	3	2	1
The student's willingness to work with different partners	4	3	2	1

Total score* _____

*Calculated by adding together all of the circled numbers.

From R.L. Clements and A. Meltzer Rady, 2012, *Urban physical education: Instructional practices and cultural activities* (Champaign, IL: Human Kinetics).

Sample Rubric 3:
Assessing a Student's Group Interactive Skills

Teacher's name: _____

Student's name: _____

Class period: _____ Grade: _____ Date: _____

Circle each appropriate score.

	4 Excellent interaction *Always*	3 Good interaction *Usually*	2 Somewhat interactive *Sometimes*	1 Poor interaction *Needs to be prompted*
The student's willingness to encourage group members to participate in new or unfamiliar physical education activities	4	3	2	1
The student's willingness to participate in group physical education activities common to different cultures	4	3	2	1
The student's willingness to advise group members not to perform activities beyond their capabilities	4	3	2	1
The student's willingness to involve all group members in the activity	4	3	2	1
The student's willingness to freely seek help from group members when needed	4	3	2	1
The student's willingness to assist group members in performing the activity	4	3	2	1
The student's willingness to modify or change some rules so that other students can fully participate	4	3	2	1
The student's willingness to congratulate group members for the successful completion of the activity	4	3	2	1
The student's willingness to participate in all group discussions	4	3	2	1
The student's willingness to socially interact with other students after the completion of the activity	4	3	2	1

Total score* _____

*Calculated by adding together all of the circled numbers.

From R.L. Clements and A. Meltzer Rady, 2012, *Urban physical education: Instructional practices and cultural activities* (Champaign, IL: Human Kinetics).

Sample Rubric 4:
Assessing the Extent to Which Objectives Have Been Achieved in a Class

Teacher's name: _____

Type of activity: _____

Class period: _____ Grade: _____ Date: _____

Circle each appropriate score.

	4 **Outstanding** *90-100% of the students achieved the objectives*	3 **Excellent** *80-89% of the students achieved the objectives*	2 **Good** *70-79% of the students achieved the objectives*	1 **Not achieved** *Less than 70% of the students achieved the objectives*
Class willingness to encourage group members to participate in new physical education activities	4	3	2	1
Class willingness to participate in group physical education activities common to different cultures	4	3	2	1
Class willingness to be attentive while an individual student or the teacher is demonstrating	4	3	2	1
Class willingness to involve all group members in the activity	4	3	2	1
Class willingness to assist non-English-speaking students	4	3	2	1
Class willingness to assist group members in performing the activity	4	3	2	1
Class willingness to modify or change some rules so that other students can fully participate	4	3	2	1
Class willingness to congratulate group members for the successful completion of the activity	4	3	2	1
Class willingness to participate in all group discussions and closure activities	4	3	2	1
Class willingness to socially interact with group members after the completion of the activity	4	3	2	1

Total score* _____

*Calculated by adding together all of the circled numbers.

From R.L. Clements and A. Meltzer Rady, 2012, *Urban physical education: Instructional practices and cultural activities* (Champaign, IL: Human Kinetics).

APPENDIX

This appendix begins with an alphabetical list of terms and definitions that can help teachers communicate with and about students from diverse settings. Following that list, the appendix gives contact information for resources that can help teachers address various social problems. Finally, the appendix presents the national standards for physical education.

A-to-Z Concepts Familiar to Urban Settings

anti-semitism—The oppression of Jewish people based on their religion or ethnic heritage.

Arab—An individual from an Arabic-speaking country; not the same as a person who is Muslim.

assimilation—Process by which an individual is absorbed into and conforms to the culture of an existing group of people.

bias—A person's preference toward persons, objects, or things that interferes with the individual's impartial judgment.

classism—Suppression of individuals because of their lower social rank or socioeconomic status.

culture—A person's learned system of beliefs, values, interests, feelings, and rules of a particular society.

Desi—An informal name for people who trace their descent to South Asia, especially India and Pakistan.

discrimination—Denying an individual access to opportunities and services on the basis of race, gender, ethnicity, religion, sexual orientation, age, or disability.

diversity—The fact or quality of being different.

equality—Fair treatment of all people without bias or favoritism.

ethnocentrism—A belief in the superiority of one's own race, ethnicity, or culture.

high-poverty school—A school having 76% to 100% of its enrollment eligible for free or reduced-price meals.

Hindi—One of the two official languages of India; should not be confused with Hindu, which is a religion practiced by many Indians.

immigrant—A person who leaves his or her country to settle in another country.

Indian—A person from or living in India.

Indochinese—People from Vietnam, Cambodia, or Laos. A more common term is Southeast Asian.

melting pot—A concept supporting the idea that foreigners should assimilate into a country's mainstream culture.

morality—Principles concerning proper and improper ways of treating other individuals.

pluralism—A concept supporting the idea that people of diverse racial, ethnic, or social groups should maintain their own culture and traditions and that differences should be valued.

popular culture—A collection of themes, attitudes, perspectives, ideas, and activities and events that are deemed well liked, in style, and acceptable by a mainstream of a culture.

prejudice—An unfavorable opinion toward a person or thing in the absence of any actual experience with that person or thing.

racially diverse—Characterizing a group of people who come from different parts of the world.

racially mixed—Referring to an individual whose ancestors came from different parts of the world.

racism—The belief that a person or a group of people are superior and therefore that it is fitting to enforce prejudices and discriminatory practices toward those deemed inferior.

Ramadan—The Islamic month of fasting. Muslims around the world abstain from all food and water from dawn to dusk for each day of this month, the ninth month of the lunar Muslim calendar.

refugee—An individual fleeing to another country due to a fear of discrimination based on his or her race, religion, social affiliation, or political ideas.

stereotype—A preconceived idea that an individual or group of people have certain group characteristics and are treated in a certain way for that reason. Stereotyping involves making generalizations that result in misunderstandings.

Title I school—A school designated under appropriate state and federal regulations as a high-poverty school that is eligible for participation in programs authorized by Title I of Public Law 107-110.

Urdu—One of the official languages of Pakistan and in many areas of India.

Suggested Resources for Social Problems Common to Adolescents

Al-Anon/Alateen
888-4AL-ANON (888-425-2666)
www.al-anon.alateen.org

American Council for Drug Education
www.acde.org

Cocaine Anonymous
310-559-5833
www.ca.org

Do It Now Foundation
480-736-0599
www.doitnow.org

Families Anonymous
800-736-9805
www.familiesanonymous.org

Hazelden
800-257-7810
www.hazelden.org

Narcotics Anonymous
818-773-9999
www.na.org

National Association of Drug Abuse Problems
212-986-1170
www.healthfinder.gov

National Cocaine Hotline
800-COCAINE
www.allaboutcounseling.com/crisis_hotlines.htm

National Council on Alcoholism and Drug Dependence (NCADD)
800-NCA-CALL (800-662-2255)
www.ncadd.org

National Families in Action
404-248-9676
www.nationalfamilies.org

National Family Partnership (National Federation of Parents for Drug-Free Youth)
800-705-8997
www.nfp.org

National Institute on Drug Abuse
301-443-1124
www.nida.nih.gov/nidahome.html

National Substance Abuse Index
877-340-0184
www.nationalsubstanceabuseindex.org

Phoenix House
800-DRUG-HELP
www.phoenixhouse.org

Pills Anonymous
www.pillsanonymous.org

Teen Drug Abuse
866-323-5611
www.teen-drug-abuse.org/resources.htm

U.S. Drug Enforcement Administration
202-307-1000
www.justice.gov/dea/index.htm

National Standards for Physical Education

Physical activity is critical to the development and maintenance of good health. The goal of physical education is to develop physically educated individuals who have the knowledge, skills, and confidence to enjoy a lifetime of healthful physical activity.

A physically educated person:

* **Standard 1:** Demonstrates competency in motor skills and movement patterns needed to perform a variety of physical activities.

* **Standard 2:** Demonstrates understanding of movement concepts, principles, strategies, and tactics as they apply to the learning and performance of physical activities.

* **Standard 3:** Participates regularly in physical activity.

* **Standard 4:** Achieves and maintains a health-enhancing level of physical fitness.

* **Standard 5:** Exhibits responsible personal and social behavior that respects self and others in physical activity settings.

* **Standard 6:** Values physical activity for health, enjoyment, challenge, self-expression, and/or social interaction.

Reprinted from National Association for Sport and Physical Education, 2004, *Moving into the future: National standards for physical education*, 2nd ed. (Reston, VA: NASPE).

BIBLIOGRAPHY

Anderson, G.F. (1969). *Knowledge and understanding in physical education.* Washington, DC: American Alliance for Health, Physical Education, Recreation and Dance.

Bennett, C.I. (1995). *Comprehensive multicultural education: Theory and practice* (3rd ed.). Allyn & Bacon.

Butt, K.L., & Pahnos, M. (1995). Why we need a multicultural focus in our schools. *Journal of Physical Education, Recreation and Dance* 66(1), 48-53.

Chase, M., Vollum, M., Toebbe, J., Clark, G., Magnotta, J., Culp, B., Schmidlein, R., & Ladda, S. (2011). Ideas exchange: What are some suggestions for overcoming any unique challenges found in urban physical education class? How might we better prepare physical educators for teaching in an urban setting? *Strategies: A Journal for Physical and Sport Educators* 23(3), 6-9.

Chepyator-Thomson, R., Xu, F., Kim, S., Schmidlein, R., & Jaekwon, J. (2008). Multiethnic diversity in kinesiology: A synthesis of literature in kinesiology-based journals (1995-2005). *ICHPER-SD Journal of Research* 3(1), 33-39.

Clements, R. (2009). Four considerations for urban physical education teachers. *Journal of Physical Education, Recreation and Dance* 80(8), 29-31.

Clements, R., & Katz-Kinzler, S. (2003). *A multicultural approach for physical education.* Champaign, IL: Human Kinetics.

Cohen, M. (2001). *Transforming the American high school.* Washington, DC: Aspen Institute.

Council of the Great City Schools. (2000). Urban school superintendents: Characteristics, tenure and salary. Second biennial survey. *Urban Indicator* 52(2), 39-51.

Culp, B. (2006). Classroom management for diverse populations. *Strategies* 20(1), 21-24.

Culp, B. (2008). Preparing qualitative studies for urban physical education environments. *Indiana Journal of Health, Physical Education, Recreation and Dance* 37(3), 33-38.

Culp, B. (2010). Are your S's in effect? Ensuring culturally responsive physical education environments. *Strategies* 24(2), 10-14.

DeVillar, R.A., Faltis, C.J., & Cummins, J.P. (Eds.). (1994). *Cultural diversity in schools: From rhetoric to practice.* Albany, NY: State University of New York Press.

Education Commission of the States. (2000). *In pursuit of quality teaching: Five key strategies for policymakers.* Denver: Education Commission of the States.

Egley, A., & Major, A.K. (2004). *Highlights of the 2002 National Youth Gang Survey.* OJJSP Fact Sheet. Washington, DC: U.S. Department of Justice.

Ellison, C.M., Boykin, A.W., Towns, D.P., & Stokes, A. (2000). *Classroom cultural ecology: The dynamics of classroom life in schools serving low-income African American children.* Washington, DC: Center for Research on the Education of Students Placed at Risk (CRESPAR), U.S. Department of Education.

Ennis, C.D., & Chen, A. (1995). Teacher's value orientation in urban and rural school settings. *Research Quarterly for Exercise and Sport* 66(1), 41-50.

Ennis, C.D., Cothran, D.J., Davison, K.S., Loftus, S.J., Owens, L., Swanson, L., & Hopsocler, P. (1997). Implementing curriculum within a context of fear and engagement. *Journal of Teaching in Physical Education* 17(1), 52-71.

Farrell, E. (1990). *Hanging in and dropping out: Voice of at-risk high school students.* New York: Teachers College Press.

Foster, H.L. (1990). *Ribbin', jivin', and playin' the dozens: The persistent dilemma in our schools* (2nd ed.). New York: Ballinger.

Fritchy, L. (2001). *Sandy "Spin" Slade: Beyond basketball.* Lawrence, MA: MasterPeace Productions. DVD.

Gay, G. (2000). *Culturally responsive teaching: Theory, research, and practice.* New York: Teachers College Press.

Griffin, P. (1985). Teaching in an urban, multiracial physical education program: The power of context. *Quest* 37(2), 154-165.

Gutierrez, K.D., & Rogoff, B. (2003). Cultural ways of learning: Individual traits or repertoires of practice? *Educational Researcher* 32(5), 19-25.

Henninger, M. (2007). Lifers and troupers: Urban physical education teachers who stay. *Journal of Teaching in Physical Education* 26(2), 125-144.

Henninger, M., & Coleman, M. (2008). De-escalation: How to take back control in your urban physical education classes. *Strategies* 21(3), 11-14.

Henninger, M., & Finch, T. (2007). Urban middle school physical education teachers: Why they stay. [Abstract]. *Research Quarterly for Exercise and Sport* 78(1), A-60.

Hunt, J. Jr. (1996). *What matters most: Teachers for America's future.* Woodbridge, VA: National Commission on Teaching and America's Future.

Hutchinson, G.E. (1995). Gender-fair teaching in physical education. *Journal of Physical Education, Recreation and Dance* 66(1), 42-47.

King, S. (1994). Winning the race against racism. *Journal of Physical Education, Recreation and Dance* 65(9), 69-74.

Kulinna, P., Cothran, D., & Regualos, R. (2006). Teachers' reports of student misbehavior in physical education. *Research Quarterly for Exercise and Sport* 77(1), 32-40.

Kulinna, P., McCaughtry, N., Cothran, D., & Martin, J. (2006). What do urban/inner-city physical education teachers teach? A contextual analysis of one elementary/primary school district. *Physical Education and Sport Pedagogy* 11(1), 45-68.

McCaughtry, N., Barnard, S., Martin, J., Shen, B., & Kulinna, P.H. (2006). Teacher's perspectives on the challenges of teaching physical education in urban schools: The student emotional filter. *Research Quarterly for Exercise and Sport* 77, 486-497.

McClafferty, K., Torres, C.A., & Mitchell, T. (Eds.). (2000). *Challenges of urban education: Sociological perspectives for the next century.* Albany, NY: State University of New York Press.

Mitchell, L.Z. (2000). A place where every teacher teaches and every student learns. *Education and Urban Society* 32(4), 506-518.

Mosston, M., & Ashworth, S. (2002). *Teaching physical education* (5th ed.). San Francisco: Benjamin Cummings.

National Association for Sport and Physical Education. (2004). *Moving into the future: National standards for physical education* (2nd ed.). Reston, VA: NASPE.

National Association for Sport and Physical Education. (2009a). *Appropriate instructional practice guidelines for high school physical education: A position statement* (3rd ed.). Reston, VA: NASPE.

National Association for Sport and Physical Education. (2009b). *Appropriate instructional practice guidelines for middle school physical education: A position statement* (3rd ed.). Reston, VA: NASPE.

Orfield, G. (2009). *Reviving the goal of an integrated society: A 21st century challenge.* Los Angeles: Civil Rights Project/Proyecto Derechos Civiles, UCLA.

Patterson, J.H., Collins, L., and Abbott, G. (2004). A study of teacher resilience in urban schools. *Journal of Instructional Psychology* 31(1), 3-11.

Perron, J., & Downey, P. (1997). Management techniques used by high school physical education teachers. *Journal of Teaching in Physical Education* 17, 72-84.

Rochkind, J., Ott, A., Immerwahr, J., Doble, J., & Johnson, J. (2008). Lessons learned: New teachers talk about their jobs, challenges, and long-range plans. Issue No. 3: Teaching in changing times. Report by the National Comprehensive Center for Teacher Quality and Public Agenda. Online at www.promoteprevent.org/resources.

Snyder, T.D., & Dillow, S.A. (2010). *Digest of education statistics 2009* (NCES 2010-013). Washington, DC: U.S. Department of Education, National Center for Education Statistics, Institute of Education Sciences.

Sparks, W.G. III. (1994). Culturally responsive pedagogy: A framework for addressing multicultural issues. *Journal of Physical Education, Recreation and Dance* 65(9), 33-36, 61.

Stanley, L.S. (1995). Multicultural questions, action research answers. *Quest* 47, 19-33.

Subramaniam, P.R., & Silverman, S. (2007). Middle school students' attitudes toward physical education. *Teaching and Teacher Education* 23, 602-611.

Supaporn, S., Dodds, P., & Griffin, L. (2003). An ecological analysis of middle school misbehavior through student and teacher perspectives. *Journal of Teaching in Physical Education* 22(3), 328-349.

Swisher, K., & Swisher, C. (1986). A multicultural physical education approach. *Journal of Physical Education, Recreation and Dance* 57(7), 35-39.

U.S. Department of Education, National Center for Education Statistics. (2008). *The condition of education 2008.* Washington, DC: National Center for Education Statistics, Institute of Education Sciences, U.S. Department of Education.

U.S. Department of Education, National Center for Education Statistics. (2010). *The condition of education 2010.* Washington, DC: National Center for Education Statistics, Institute of Education Sciences, U.S. Department of Education.

Wakefield, D.B., Talbert, B.A., & Pense, S. (2006). A descriptive study on the preparation of student teachers to work with diverse populations. *Online Journal for Workforce Education and Development* 2(1). Retrieved August 20, 2011, from http://wed.siu.edu/Journal/.

Ward, P., & O'Sullivan, M. (2006). The contexts of urban settings. *Journal of Teaching in Physical Education* 25(4), 348-362.

Wepner, S. (2009). From the dean's perspective: Life informs art and the art of teaching. *Manhattanville College, Purchase, NY, School of Education Newsletter for Faculty, Administration, and Staff* 6(1), 1-3.

Wright, P., & Burton, S. (2008, April). Implementation and outcomes of a responsibility-based physical activity program integrated into an intact high school physical education class. *Journal of Teaching in Physical Education* 27(2), 138-154. Retrieved February 15, 2009, from www.tpsr-alliance.org/documents/dr-wright1.pdf.

Villegas, A.M., & Lucas, T. (2002). *Educating culturally responsive teachers: A coherent approach.* Albany, NY: State University of New York Press.

Zeng, H.Z., Hipscher, M., & Leung, R. (2011). Attitudes of high school students towards physical education and their sport activity preferences. *Journal of Social Sciences* 7(4), 529-537.

INDEX

ABOUT THE AUTHORS

Rhonda L. Clements, EdD, is a professor and the director of the master of arts in teaching (MAT) in physical education and sport pedagogy graduate program at Manhattanville College in Purchase, New York, where she conducts research and teaches about historical and sociocultural issues in sport and physical education.

Clements is the author of nine books on movement, play, and games. She is past president of the American Association for the Child's Right to Play, a UN-recognized association composed of experts in play, games, and sports in 49 countries. The association's primary purpose is to protect, preserve, and promote play and leisure activities throughout the world.

Clements has written numerous articles related to physical education, including 20 on sport and play factors. She is also a consultant for numerous manufacturers of sport equipment and toys and has been interviewed by more than 300 journalists regarding children's right to leisure and physical play. She has presented at 40 international or national conferences and over 60 state or local conferences on topics related to cultural understanding through play and sport. Clements lives in New York City.

Amy Meltzer Rady, EdD, is an assistant professor in the department of kinesiology at a state university in New Jersey. In addition to her teaching responsibilities in movement education and curriculum and teaching physical education in secondary schools, she regularly observes teachers and supervises student teachers in New Jersey's public schools.

Rady has extensive experience teaching physical education activity classes at Barnard College of Columbia University in New York and at the SUNY at Stony Brook. She has also taught physical education in public and private schools, most recently in the Scarsdale Public Schools of Westchester, New York.

Rady has presented at the National Association of Kinesiology and Physical Education in Higher Education Conference; the Eastern District Association of the American Alliance for Health, Physical Education, Recreation and Dance (AAHPERD); and the state conference of the New Jersey Association for Health, Physical Education, Recreation and Dance. Her presentations focus on multicultural activities and urban activities. Rady has expertise in Project Adventure and cooperative learning experiences.

Both authors are longtime members of AAHPERD and their state and local physical education associations, and both serve on the National Association for Sport and Physical Education (NASPE) Diversity and Inclusiveness Task Force.